C.G. JUNG
Lord of the Underworld

Other books by Colin Wilson:

FRANKENSTEIN'S CASTLE
INTRODUCTION TO THE NEW EXISTENTIALISM
MYSTERIES
NEW PATHWAYS IN PSYCHOLOGY
THE OCCULT
ORIGINS OF THE SEXUAL IMPULSE
THE OUTSIDER
QUEST FOR WILHELM REICH
STRANGE POWERS
THE WAR AGAINST SLEEP: The Philosophy of Gurdjieff
RUDOLF STEINER: The Man and his Vision
ALEISTER CROWLEY: The Nature of the Beast

C.G. JUNG

Lord of the Underworld

Colin Wilson

THE AQUARIAN PRESS
Wellingborough, Northamptonshire

First published 1984
This paperback edition 1988

British Library Cataloguing in Publication Data

Wilson, Colin, *1931-*
[Lord of the underworld] C. G. Jung: Lord of the underworld.
1. Jung, C. G.
[Lord of the underworld] I. Title
150.19'54   BF173.J85

ISBN 0-85030-716-3

*The Aquarian Press is part of the Thorsons Publishing Group,
Wellingborough, Northamptonshire, NN8 2RQ, England*

Printed in Great Britain by Biddles Limited, Guildford, Surrey

2   4   6   8   10   9   7   5   3   1

Contents

Acknowledgements

I wish to thank Messrs Routledge and Kegan Paul for their permission to quote from Jung's Collected Works, and from the other volumes by Jung listed in the bibliography. I also wish to thank Aldus Books for their permission to quote from Jung's *Man and His Symbols*. I am grateful to Israel Regardie for sending me a copy of Spiegelman's book *The Knight*. My thanks to my old friend Vincent Brome for permission to quote from his lively biography of Jung.

Introduction

Jung was sixty-eight years old when, taking his daily walk, he slipped on an icy road and broke his ankle. A few days later he suffered a severe heart attack. In hospital, he was kept alive with oxygen and camphor injections; his nurse told him later that he had been surrounded by a kind of glow that she had noticed around the dying.

In this state, Jung seems to have experienced the sort of visions that have often been described by people who have hovered between life and death. The first was of the earth seen from about a thousand miles up in space, with the sea and the continents bathed in a blue light; he could make out the reddish-yellow desert of Arabia, and the snow-covered Himalayas. Then, nearby, he saw an immense block of stone, like a meteorite; but it had been hollowed out, like certain temples he had seen in India. Near the entrance, a Hindu sat in the lotus position. As he approached, Jung says: 'I had the feeling that everything was being sloughed away; everything I aimed at or wished for or thought, the whole phantasmagoria of earthly existence, fell away or was stripped from me — an extremely painful process.' And as he was led by the Hindu to an inner temple, full of burning wicks, he had a certainty that he was about to meet 'all those people to whom I belong in reality', and that he would suddenly understand the meaning of his life, and why he had been sent into the world.

Then, from the direction of Europe, something floated up towards him; he recognized the doctor who was treating him; but he had been transformed into the image of an ancient ruler of Kos, the site of the temple of Aesculapius, the god of healing. The doctor explained that Jung would not be allowed to die — that at least thirty women were protesting at the idea of his leaving the earth. Jung felt a deep sense of disappointment as the vision faded. Like so many others who have been convinced that they have died briefly, then been recalled to life, he felt resentful at being forced to return.

Because the doctor had appeared to him in the form of an ancient king, Jung was convinced that he was going to die — in fact, that the doctor's death would be a substitute for his own. On 4 April 1944, the first day Jung was allowed to sit up in bed, the doctor took to his own bed with a fever and died shortly afterwards of septicaemia. Jung was his last patient.

It was a time of visions: 'Night after night I floated in a state of purest bliss.' As morning approached he would feel: 'Now grey morning is coming again; now comes the grey world with its boxes.' And, as he became physically stronger, the visions ceased. Jung did not regard them as some form of dream or hallucination, but as insights into the basic reality. 'It was not a product of imagination. The visions and experiences were utterly real; there was nothing subjective about them; they all had a quality of absolute objectivity.'

Jung was to live on for another seventeen years. But the near-death experience had caused a profound change in his outlook. Throughout his working life, Jung had felt obliged to protect himself by presenting himself to the world as a scientist. Not long after his recovery, he was writing to a correspondent who was trying to convert him to Catholicism: 'My dear Sir! My pursuit is science, not apologetics and not philosophy. My interest is scientific, yours evangelical.' Yet anyone who is familiar with Jung's work knows that this is a half-truth; Jung *was* both a philosopher and an evangelist. But the near-death experience seems to have made him less defensive about presenting his deepest convictions, less concerned about being accused of stepping beyond the limits of science. One of the most startling results was his introduction to the Richard Wilhelm version of the *I Ching*, written in 1949. Jung had been familiar with the Chinese oracle since 1920, when he had spent the summer making 'an all-out attack on the riddle of the book'. He had made a number of references to it in works written after that date, but always brief and non-commital. But in the 1949 introduction he speaks openly about consulting the oracle by

means of the coin method, 'asking its judgement about
. . . my intention to present it to the Western mind', and
analyzing the oracle's reply in some detail. He had been
consulting the *I Ching* since 1920; this was the first time he
had dared to admit to it. He also admits that there is no
possible 'scientific' defence for taking it seriously. Nevertheless, he is prepared to do so, and dismisses criticism
with the comment: 'The less one thinks about the theory
of the *I Ching*, the more soundly one sleeps.'

In 1950, one of Jung's most baffling and difficult works,
Aion, included chapters on the prophecies of Nostradamus and sections on Gnostic and Qabalistic ideas that
sometimes read as if they came from some sixteenth-
century treatise on magic. In the following year, at the
Eranos conference, Jung delivered his paper *On Synchronicity*, justifying astrology and the *I Ching* by appealing to
the concept of 'meaningful coincidence'; in an expanded
version of the paper, he begins by admitting that he has
now 'made good a promise which for many years I lacked
the courage to fulfil'. In 1954 came Jung's most deeply
personal book, *Answer to Job*, his own highly controversial
attempt to 'justify the ways of God to man'. The scientist
had at last ceased to pretend that he was neither a
philosopher nor an evangelist. And yet the result was not
denunciation by colleagues or the accusation that he was
becoming senile. It was the kind of acclaim that he had
never experienced in the years when he felt he was doing
his most important work. Jung suddenly became the guru
of the Western world, a universal oracle who was
bracketed with Gandhi and Albert Schweitzer. He was
probably more responsible than anyone for the surge of
interest in 'occultism' — in the paranormal and Eastern
religious disciplines — that began soon after his death in
1961. The title of one of the most popular encylopedias of
this period, *Man, Myth and Magic*, might have been taken
from one of Jung's own works.

Now, in retrospect, we can see that Jung was never the
scientist he wanted to be taken for, and that this makes no
difference to his greatness. One of his biographers, the
psychologist Anthony Storr, writes: 'It is easy to lose
patience with Jung . . . More especially, I find it difficult to
sympathise with his preoccupation with the occult; with
his views on synchronicity, and with the ghosts and

poltergeists which throng his autobiography.' Storr wants
to see Jung purely as a scientist, as Freud's greatest
successor. But it is a hopeless task. For we have to
recognize that, from the very beginning, Jung was
obsessed with the occult. (The word, after all, means
simply 'hidden', so it should not be necessary to apologize
for it by putting it in inverted commas.) His childhood and
teens were full of conflict between religion and agnostic-
ism. A drowned body fished out of the river when he was
four produced a lifelong preoccupation with corpses. As a
student, he read every book he could find on spiritualistic
phenomena. Two curious poltergeist incidents happened
in his own home.* His cousin Hélène Preiswerk, a girl of
fifteen, developed mediumistic powers, and Jung
attended a number of seances, complete with table-
rapping and the movements of a glass. Several different
personalities spoke through his cousin, including a number of dead relatives. Yet when Jung came to write this up
for his inaugural dissertation, he called it 'On the
Psychology and Pathology of So-Called Occult Phenomena', and treated it primarily as a case of 'multiple
personality' due to hysteria and sexual repression. But by
then he was first assistant physician in the Burghölzli
Clinic, and had discovered Freud's *Interpretation of Dreams*.

What emerges very clearly from the early chapters of
Jung's autobiography, *Memories, Dreams, Reflections*, is that
he was an introverted romantic who dreamed of beautiful
girls and heroic actions, and that his interest in spiritualism was an attempt to find a mode of intensity that could
displace the boredom and triviality of everyday life. It
arouses echoes of the young W.B. Yeats, who also
attended seances and became a member of the magical
Order of the Golden Dawn and a disciple of Madame
Blavatsky. And the parallel with Yeats makes us aware of
the more general problem of the romantic in a world
apparently designed for realists. Yeats turned to a dream
world of ancient Ireland, of fairies, heroes and supernatural beings. But in a poem of old age, 'The Circus Animals'
Desertion', he is cynical about this substitute reality. He
asks where these 'masterful images' had their origin, and

*See p. 29.

replies: in 'a mound of refuse or the sweepings of the street'. He sees his imagination as a kind of ladder that he climbs to escape reality, and concludes:

> Now that my ladder's gone
> I must lie down where all the ladders start,
> In the foul rag-and-bone shop of the heart.

These are perhaps the most profoundly pessimistic lines ever written by a major poet. They imply that romantic ideals are a flight from 'ordinariness', which is bound to end in failure, since the ordinariness is real and the ideals are not. But this is not simply a problem for romantic idealists. Every human being is born into the world with the same feeling of weakness, of helplessness, of passivity. If he is unfortunate enough to be surrounded by people who lack intelligence and imagination — a fairly likely contingency, since this description covers most of the human race — then the weakness will be compounded by a feeling of inevitability, a tacit conviction that things *are* as they are, and no change can be expected. Yeats's reaction to this situation was to turn inward, into a world of fantasy. Like all poets, he wanted to shatter the world to pieces and 'rebuild it nearer to the heart's desire'. Since this was impossible, he concentrated on creating his own vision of a 'land of heart's desire' in poetry and drama. But he saw this vision as a mere escape from a world he detested — hence the comment about the 'foul rag-and-bone shop of the heart'.

Jung, starting from a very similar background, was luckier than Yeats. He also looked for an alternative to 'ordinariness' in the world of the occult and paranormal. But at this point he became fascinated by the equally strange, gothic world of mental illness. He explains in his autobiography that this happened quite suddenly when he opened Krafft-Ebing's *Textbook of Psychiatry*, with its introductory comment that 'It is probably due to the peculiarity of the subject and its incomplete state of development that psychiatric textbooks are stamped with a more-or-less subjective character.' And when he read, a few lines further on, that psychoses are 'diseases of the personality', his heart began to pound, and he had to stand up to draw a deep breath. Why should these straightforward comments have produced such excitement? First of all, the admission that psychiatry is *subjective* because it is undeveloped — an indication that it would have the room for the subjective approach of a romantic idealist, and that therefore he could take his place among its pioneers. But the phrase 'diseases of the personality' also evokes the whole world of *fin de siècle* world-rejection, of alcoholic painters and *poètes maudits* like Baudelaire and Verlaine. Jung had actually taken a course in psychiatry when he read these words, but had found it uninspiring. What excited him was the notion that this 'undeveloped' field offered an outlet for his own dammed creative energies.

So while Yeats continued to be a poet and an ineffectual Irish nationalist, Jung came to terms with the real world as a scientist. And as a champion of the controversial ideas of Freud, he had soon acquired an international reputation. This might be regarded as a *volte face* — the poacher turning gamekeeper because it provides more security. But in fact, Jung's therapeutic practice soon began to provide him with evidence for the actual existence of that 'other reality' that so obsessed Yeats — and in which Yeats had never been able wholly to believe. When a patient committed suicide by blowing out his brains, Jung awoke in the middle of the night with a dull pain as if a bullet had entered his forehead. During an argument with Freud about occultism, Jung produced poltergeist effects — loud explosions in a bookcase. A dream of 1909 convinced Jung of the existence of the 'collective unconscious', some common foundation of all human psychic experience. In 1910, he began to accumulate evidence that this collective unconscious contains certain basic magical and religious symbols, and that 'there are archaic psychic components which have entered the individual psyche'. The break with Freud was followed by a period of mental upheaval in which he found he could descend — while wide awake — into his own unconscious mind, and converse with beings he met there as if they were real people. One day when he asked himself 'Is this really science I am doing', a woman's voice from inside himself answered: 'No, it is art'; as a result, Jung became convinced of the existence of the 'alternative' sub-personality, the anima (or, in women, animus). For the rest of his life he continued to have experiences — like the vision of the earth, followed by the death of his doctor — that convinced him that there *is* another level of reality beyond the merely physical. In the final chapter of his autobiography he writes: 'The validity of such terms as mana, daimon or God can be neither disproved nor affirmed. We can, however, establish that the sense of strangeness connected with the experience of something objective, apparently outside the psyche, is indeed authentic.' In that sense, he was luckier than Yeats, who could never quite bring himself to believe that man's visions and dreams are more than an attempt to escape the dreariness of physical reality.

Yet for most of his life, Jung preferred to remain silent about these convictions. Was this cowardice? He himself would have said it was simply a determination to maintain a healthy scientific scepticism. Nevertheless, the results of this scepticism could at times look very like dishonesty. In 1919, he published in the *Proceedings of the Society for Psychical Research* a paper entitled 'The Psychological Foundation of Belief in Spirits', in which spirits are explained as 'projections' of the unconscious mind. In the summer of the following year, Jung rented a weekend cottage near London that proved to be haunted. There were knockings, dripping noises, and unpleasant smells. A large animal seemed to be rushing around the bedroom. One night, as a storm of blows rained on the walls, Jung opened his eyes to see half a head — of an old woman — on the pillow beside him. A colleague who had rented the cottage was sceptical about the haunting, but left hurriedly after spending a sleepless night with footsteps walking around him. The cottage finally had to be pulled down as unsaleable. So by 1920, Jung knew that ghosts cannot be explained as manifestations of the unconscious. In 1948, he wrote a postscript to his article on belief in spirits, admitting that his earlier views were inadequate, yet stating that he could not answer the question of whether spirits really exist as independent entities 'because I am not in a position to adduce experiences that would prove it one way or the other'. And it was two more years before he finally told the story about the haunted cottage in a contribution to a book by Fanny Moser called *Ghosts: Reality or Delusion?* Jung found it very difficult to relax the stance of the hard-headed scientist and state his convictions openly.

But at least he decided to do so at precisely the right moment. By the 1950s, the new generation felt a need to break away from the obsessive political preoccupations of the past two decades. In America, the Beat Generation talked about freedom and Zen and the need to 'drop out'. In England, 'Angry Young Men' expressed the same spirit of individual protest. Aldous Huxley's *Doors of Perception* advocated the use of psychedelic drugs to 'expand consciousness'. The result was a muddled spirit of revolt with no particular aim. Jung was able to offer this movement some kind of purpose and direction based on the result of fifty years of reflection on the strange forces of the unconscious. Although he himself strenuously denied that he should be regarded as a prophet or a preacher, he was, in fact, providing something very like a system of religious beliefs. While fashionable theologians talked about the 'death of God', Jung was asserting that the collective unconscious provides us with evidence of another order of reality. Bertrand Russell had written in 1918: 'I *must*, before I die, find *some* way to say the essential thing that is in me, that I have never said yet — a thing that is not love or hate or pity or scorn, but the very breath of life, fierce and coming from far away, bringing into human life the vastness and fearful passionless force of non-human things . . . ' This is a statement of the essence of religious belief: the conviction that there is something far *bigger* than human beings, and that man is capable of opening himself to this greater force. But Russell said this in a private letter, and kept it out of his books on philosophy and education. Jung stated a similar conviction again and again in the last years of his life. 'We know that something unknown, alien, does come our way, just as we know that we do not ourselves *make* a dream or an inspiration . . . ' It was this powerful conviction of the strangeness of the universe, and the immense complexity of the collective unconscious, that lent his work the inspirational force that turned him, in the last decade of his life, into the 'sage of Küsnacht'.

Jung had a lifelong admiration for Goethe — of whom he believed himself a descendant — and in his creative development he seems to have been as fortunate as Goethe: the early acclaim, the slow leisurely development under propitious circumstances, the final rich harvest of insights in old age. Yet there is another aspect of Jung that can be traced throughout his life: a curious passion for obscurity, for ambiguity. He was known as a brilliant conversationalist and a fine spontaneous lecturer; this can be seen in lectures like *The Vision Seminars*. Yet the style of his books is Germanic and obscure, as if he is afraid to submit his meaning to easy scrutiny. When, shortly before his death, he was approached by a British publisher with a suggestion for a book on his ideas for the general reader, Jung refused flatly, explaining that he had always been distrustful of this idea of popularization. A dream changed his mind, and the result was *Man and his Symbols*; but the reluctance seems to have sprung from the same source as his unwillingness to talk about his 'occultism' before the late 1940s. The explanation may be that, while Jung's life work was an attempt to establish the existence of another order of reality, his scientific training made him long for a concrete foundation on which to base his convictions. And he was never quite satisfied with the foundation. The near-death experience convinced him that it had to be now or never; but he never seems to have been quite happy with his new exposed position. He became subject to a kind of depression, writing to Laurens van der Post: 'I am an increasingly lonely old man writing for other lonely men'. And in the last paragraph of his autobiography he states: 'It seems to me that the aliena-tion which has so long separated me from the world has become transferred to my own inner world, and has revealed to me an unexpected unfamiliarity with myself.'

'An unexpected unfamiliarity with myself.' The phrase is highly revealing. Socrates' 'Know thyself' could be regarded as the guiding principle of Jung's life work. As a psychoanalyst, his aim was to become familiar with the unknown corners of his being. He certainly struck other people as a man who was at peace with himself because he had achieved self-knowledge Yet the attempt, in those later years, to crystallize his deepest convictions only seemed to crack the foundations he had taken so much trouble to reinforce. He had spent his life trying to be a scientist — the man whose role, according to T.H. Huxley, is to sit down before fact like a little child, and to follow humbly wherever she leads. When Jung expressed his belief that the *I Ching* should be taken seriously, he was following this precept, and stating what he saw as a fact. But one of the main difficulties of the world of the paranormal is that once an investigator has expressed cautious acceptance of any one aspect of it, he finds it almost impossible to stay within his chosen limits. New facts keep presenting themselves, and as he keeps on stretching his theory to accommodate them, he realizes that the theory is finally going to explode like an overblown balloon. Jung was in the same position once he had committed himself to the idea of synchronicity. Synchronicity is meaningful coincidence, and it either implies that 'powers' outside us are organizing coincidences to draw our attention to new facts, or that the unconscious mind itself can somehow influence matter. Jung wrote: 'Either there are physical processes which cause psychic happenings, or there is a pre-existent psyche which organises matter.' The same theory is implied in his earlier notion of 'exteriorization phenomena', like the explosions he caused in Freud's bookcase when they were arguing about occultism.

But if the mind can somehow organize events, then why are we living in a world that is obviously so far from 'the heart's desire'? Jung, like Yeats, had spent his life wrestling with that question; and just as he seemed to have established, to his own satisfaction, that man is not merely a biological accident in a meaningless universe, he let the genie out of the bottle again with a question that seemed to put him back to square one. 'No language is adequate to this paradox', he remarks gloomily towards the end of his autobiography. And the curiously pessimistic and inconclusive tone of these final pages certainly seems to suggest a task that has been left unfinished.

But then, a man's biography may provide answers that he himself would have been incapable of formulating.

One

A Dual Personality

As a young man, Jung struck people as breezy and full of self-confidence; others found him aggressive, tactless and domineering. Ideas flowed from him in an endless stream, and he had a range of laughs varying from an infectious chuckle to a Homeric boom. He was undoubtedly what zoologists call an alpha, a highly dominant individual. This represented a remarkable feat of self-transformation, for as a child he was shy, nervous and introverted. One schoolfriend who met him at about the age of four remembered the meeting because 'I had never come across such an a-social monster before'. Jung suffered from nervous eczema and was accident-prone; on one occasion he had to have several stitches in a cut on his scalp. He also fell downstairs, and almost slipped from a bridge into the Rhine Falls, being snatched back just in time by a maid. 'These things', he wrote, 'point to an unconscious suicidal urge, or, it may be, to a fatal resistance to life in this world.'

Carl Gustav Jung was born on 26 July 1875 at Kesswil, a village on the shores of Lake Constance. Most boys tend to model themselves on their fathers, and it was Jung's misfortune that his father, the Revd Paul Jung, was a nonentity, an undistinguished clergyman who suffered from religious doubts, quarrelled with his wife, and never lived up to his early promise as a brilliant linguist. Dominance seems to have skipped a generation, for Jung's grandfather, after whom he was named, was a famous man in the city of Basle, a successful doctor, a prominent Freemason, and Rector of the University. There was a family legend that he was the illegitimate grandson of Goethe. Jung never had a chance to model himself on his grandfather, who died eleven years before he was born.

Jung's mother, *née* Emilie Preiswerk, seems to have

been an altogether stronger character. Daughter of a professor of Hebrew, she is described by one source as fat, ugly, authoritarian and haughty. Even her son said she was down-to-earth and commonplace. When he was three, she seems to have had some kind of mental breakdown, probably due to marital difficulties, and was hospitalized for several months. The child felt deserted — this was the period he developed nervous eczema — and said that from then on he always felt mistrustful when the word 'love' was uttered. 'Woman' seemed basically unreliable. His father was reliable, but ineffectual. It was not an ideal background for the development of self-confidence.

It became even worse when he was sent to school in Basle, at the age of eleven. Among well-dressed boys who spent their holidays in the Alps or by the sea, he became aware of his family's poverty, and began to feel sorry for his father — hardly an attitude to increase his own self-confidence. He hated mathematics and found divinity classes unspeakably dull. At some point, he was the victim of a sexual assault by a man he worshipped — an episode he later confessed to Freud, but without adding any further details. He continued to be accident-prone, and there were attempts to bully him by the other boys — fortunately, he was becoming big and strong.

The most significant event of his early life occurred when he was twelve. In the cathedral square, a boy shoved him so violently that he fell and struck his head on the pavement, becoming momentarily unconscious. He lay there longer than necessary to worry his assailant, and the thought flashed through his head 'Now I shan't have to go to school any more.' People picked him up and took him to a house nearby where two aunts lived. The accident reinforced his self-pity. He began having fainting spells, and was allowed to stay away from school for six months. His parents worried and consulted doctors; the boy was sent off to relatives in Winterthur, where he intensely enjoyed hanging around the railway station. It was suggested that he was suffering from epilepsy.

Back home again, he was hiding behind a shrub in the garden one day when he heard a visitor ask after his health; his father replied: 'It's a sad business . . . they think it may be epilepsy. It would be dreadful if it were incurable. I have lost what little I had, and what will become of the boy if he cannot earn his own living?'

The words deeply disturbed Jung: pity for his father, self-pity, fear of poverty, all mingled together. He had wasted six months. He hurried off to his father's study, took out his Latin grammar, and began to work. After a short time he had a fainting fit and fell off the chair. He refused to stop working. Soon another attack came; he refused to give up and went on studying. After an hour, he experienced a third fainting fit. Still he pressed on grimly. Then, suddenly, he felt better than he had felt since the attacks began. And then they suddenly ceased. Jung was able to go back to school.

In recounting this episode in his autobiography he merely comments, 'I had learned what neurosis is.' But there was far more to it than that. What Jung had done, with the aid of the bang on the head, was to induce a more or less instantaneous *habit*. It was, in effect, a form of self-hypnosis. Just as we can induce in ourselves a prickling of the scalp when we listen to a favourite piece of music, Jung had learned to induce fainting spells when faced with stress. He had enlisted the aid of the 'robot' that lives in the depths of the mind to help him evade the boredom and misery of school. He had chosen the route of illness and escape — the route chosen by so many of the nineteenth-century romantics. Overhearing his father's anxious comments recalled him to a sense of responsibility. What he then did was to deliberately *outface* and overcome the habit. He was saying, in effect: 'I caused it; I can get rid of it.' So at the age of twelve, Jung had not merely grasped the basic mechanism of neurosis: he had recognized that it can be cured by an *act of will*. This could well have been the most important experience of his life; it was certainly a turning point.

The experience taught Jung to have done with self-pity. 'I knew . . . that the whole affair was a diabolical plot on my part. I knew, too, that it was never going to happen again.' He flung himself into his studies, often working until three in the morning, and rising at five. He was ashamed of what had happened, yet he could see why it had happened: because of his love of nature, his love of being alone. It had almost betrayed him into lifelong invalidism — as it had betrayed his eminent contemporary

Marcel Proust. It had been a narrow escape.

The reward came in the form of a semi-mystical experience. 'I was taking the long road to school from Klein-Hüningen, where we lived, to Basel, when suddenly for a single moment I had the overwhelming impression of having just emerged from a dense cloud. I knew all at once: now I am *myself!* It was as if a wall of mist were at my back, and behind that wall there was not yet an "I". But at this moment *I came upon myself.* Previously I had existed too, but everything had merely happened to me. Now I happened to myself. Now I knew: I am myself now, I exist. Previously I had been willed to do this and that: now *I* willed. This experience seemed to me tremendously important and new: there was "authority" in me.'

Jung had made another fundamental discovery. When human beings spend their lives doing the will of others, they could be compared to crabs, a creature that has its skeleton outside. Inside, it is soft. The moment a man feels inspired to do his own will, he turns into a vertebrate, a creature with its skeleton *inside.* Suddenly, he has a backbone. In our society, few people evolve from crabs into vertebrates, for we become accustomed to doing the will of others from the moment we are born. Jung's struggle to overcome the habit of defeat had made him aware that he was a vertebrate.

At school, before the 'accident', Jung had carved a kind of manikin out of a ruler. He had placed it in a pencil case, together with an oblong black stone from the Rhine, painted in two colours, and hidden it on a beam in the attic. It was his symbol of his secret soul. During his period of illness, he had forgotten all about the manikin in the attic. He notes in his autobiography that this new feeling of 'authority' was analogous to the feeling of value inspired by the manikin in the pencil case.

Now, with this new sense of his own value, Jung recognized that he was two persons. When a friend's father lost his temper with him for behaving irresponsibly in a boat, he felt enraged that this fat, ignorant boor dared to insult him, yet at the same time, could see that the man's anger was justified; it was the schoolboy who was being told off, and the 'man of authority' who was enraged.

In fact, Jung had already become convinced that this

'man of authority' was an old man who lived in the eighteenth century and wore buckled shoes and a white wig. This conviction had come upon him one day when an antique green carriage drove past their house, and he had experienced an odd feeling: 'That comes from *my* times.' And in the house of his aunts — to which he had been carried when he fainted — there was a statuette of a well-known character from eighteenth-century Basle, a Dr Stückelberger, who wore buckled shoes; again, Jung had the curious certainty that these shoes were his own. Possibly he was acquainted with the story that his grandfather was Goethe's illegitimate son, and was identifying with Goethe. Whatever the cause, he began to experience himself as a dual personality, living in two ages simultaneously.

Jung seems to have been a conventionally religious boy, and this is understandable, since he was the son of a clergyman, and Switzerland in the nineteenth century was a highly conventional place, as stiff and correct as those Norwegian towns in Ibsen's plays. In his early teens, he experienced a religious crisis. It began one day when he came out of school and saw the sun sparkling on the tiles of the cathedral roof. He was struck by the thought that it was a beautiful world that God had created, and that He must be sitting on His throne in the blue sky. This thought was followed by a feeling of terror. It was only after several sleepless nights that he realized what had caused the terror: the incipient thought of a large turd falling from under the throne and shattering the roof. As soon as he realized what had caused him so much alarm, he experienced tremendous relief. Again, it was like a mini-lesson in psychoanalysis: the thought that had tried to struggle out of the subconscious, and been promptly repressed, and the relief that followed the decision not to suppress it any more.

This was not the end of the religious crisis. Now he had begun to think about God, he wanted to know the answers to certain questions. These were the same questions that had caused Gautama, the Buddha, to become a monk: the mystery of human suffering, of disease and old age and death. He tried to find the answers in a book called *Christian Dogmatics* in his father's library, and decided that it was drivel. That meant that his father had been taken in by the drivel, and had wasted his life. He tried discussing his doubts with his father, and concluded that his father also suffered from doubts. The experience of his first communion convinced him finally that he was no longer a believer. In his mid-teens he discovered Goethe's *Faust* and Schopenhauer's *World as Will and Illusion*, and was deeply moved and excited by both. They treated life as something profound and tragic. Schopenhauer led him to Kant. He became a voracious reader; his father said: 'The boy is interested in *everything* — but heaven knows where he'll end up.' An essay he wrote on Faust seemed so adult that the teacher refused to believe that he had written it. His schoolfriends pulled his leg about his interest in philosophy, and nicknamed him 'Father Abraham'. He was not entirely displeased with the nickname; it showed a certain penetration.

He labelled the two halves of his personality Number 1 and Number 2. Number 1 was the schoolboy, the part that was in contact with the external world; Number 2 was the wise old man. As he grew older, Number 1 became increasingly interested in science — particularly after a holiday at Entlebuch, where he met a chemist who 'understood the secret of stones'. (Jung mentioned that he revered him, and it seems conceivable that this was the man responsible for the sexual assault that so shocked him.) In studying science, he found that his self-doubt was banished. Another experience of this period was equally important. He went on a visit to a distillery, sampled various strong drinks, and ended in a delightful state of drunkenness. To his astonishment, he realized that all feeling of self-division had vanished, and that he experienced a marvellous sense of strength and affirmation. In spite of a hangover, he remembered the experience as an insight into beauty and meaning — a discovery that has produced many an alcoholic.

Another experience brought a premonition of release. He travelled back home with his father, via Lucerne, and went on a steamship for the first time. At Vitznau, he went to the top of a mountain in a small locomotive, and, on the peak, again experienced a tremendous sense of delight and relief. 'I no longer knew what was bigger — I or the mountain . . . This was the best and most precious gift my father had ever given me.'

One windy day, walking to school beside the Rhine, he saw a sailing vessel running before the storm and went into a daydream about a medieval town on a lake, surmounted by a fortified castle on a rock. (Significantly, Yeats had also daydreamed of a castle on a rock.) He, Jung, lived in the castle, and was the Justice of the Peace and arbitrator in the town. The most important place in the castle was the keep, in whose tower there was a copper column that ramified into fine branches, which somehow conducted an energy from the air down into the cellar — Jung's laboratory, in which he made gold by the use of this energy. For months, the walk to and from the school was shortened by delightful fantasies about the town and the castle. Then, typically, he grew sick of the daydream, and began working out how to build a real castle; he made models out of mud and stones. Once again, without realizing it, he had symbolically lived through the basic experience of the nineteenth-century romantic poets, and emerged from dreams into reality. The Number 1 personality was becoming strong enough to face the world.

This was just as well, for Jung was reaching the age when he had to begin to think about a career. And for the son of a poverty-stricken Protestant pastor, this was an immense problem. He would have liked to become an archaeologist; but there was no department of archaeology in Basle. The next choice was zoology — he was fascinated by animals and birds; but this could only qualify him to become a schoolmaster or an assistant in a zoological garden. The idea of becoming a pastor like his father was completely out of the question. The only career that had any sort of appeal was medicine — his grandfather's profession. It was not that Jung felt he had any vocation for medicine; merely that it would at least enable him to study science.

There was not even any certainty that he could attend university in Basle; his father could not afford it. His father applied to the university for a grant, and Jung was astonished and ashamed when it was approved; he was ashamed because he was quite convinced that the university authorities disliked him. He mentions on a number of occasions that he possessed a personality that aroused dislike among schoolteachers and fellow students, but fails to explain why this was so. The explanation can be found in a passage in which Bernard Shaw speaks about his own early manhood: 'When a young man has achieved nothing and is doing nothing, and when he is obviously so poor that he ought to be doing something very energetically, it is rather trying to find him assuming an authority in conversation and an equality in terms which only conspicuous success and distinguished ability could make becoming. Yet this is what is done, quite unconsciously, by young persons who have in them the potentiality of such success and ability.'* Jung was striving to develop his 'Number 1' personality, and his unconscious self-assertiveness must have aroused irritation.

At this point in his life — at the beginning of his university career — Jung was painfully aware of the contrast between his 'two personalities'. 'Through Number 1's eyes I saw myself as a rather disagreeable and moderately gifted young man with vaulting ambitions, an undisciplined temperament, and dubious manners, alternating between naive enthusiasm and fits of childish disappointment, in his innermost essence a hermit and obscurantist. On the other hand, No. 2 regarded No. 1 as a difficult and thankless moral task, a lesson that had to be got through somehow, complicated by various faults such as spells of laziness, despondency, depression, inept enthusiasm for ideas and things that nobody valued, liable to imaginary friendships, limited, prejudiced, stupid . . . ' Since discovering Goethe, Jung had become inclined to identify this Number 2 personality with Faust.

If Jung had been fortunate enough to stumble upon a book by a remarkable American writer, Thomson Jay Hudson, called *The Law of Psychic Phenomena* (1893), he would undoubtedly have arrived at a deeper understanding of his two personalities and their relationship to one another. Hudson, a newspaper editor, had become fascinated by hypnosis, and the unusual powers that it seemed able to release in hypnotized subjects. Hudson made the interesting suggestion that man has two 'minds', which he called the objective mind and the subjective mind. The objective mind is the part of us that looks out towards the external world, the part that 'copes', the realist. The

*Preface to *Immaturity*.

subjective mind looks inward, and is concerned with feelings, sensations, emotions. Hudson's most important realization is that we all 'identify' with the objective mind; we feel that this is 'us'. The subjective mind remains in abeyance, hidden in shadow, so to speak. Under hypnosis, the objective mind is put to sleep, and the subjective mind is free to express itself. It may, for example, display astonishing powers of recall, conjuring up detailed memories of childhood, or show unusual intellectual or artistic creativity. In one remarkable case of the 1890s, recorded by Theodore Flournoy, a young woman in trance described in detail an earlier 'incarnation' as a Hindu princess, and visits to the planet Mars, with astonishing details of its cities, its inhabitants and its language. Hudson argued that the powers of the 'subjective mind' are far more astonishing than we realize — that, for example, it is capable of telepathy, and of healing people at a distance — even thousands of miles. In fact, Hudson was convinced that the miracles of Jesus were simply due to the unusually close accord between his objective and subjective minds.

Hudson's book created a sensation in America in the 1890s; unfortunately, it does not seem to have reached Basle. It would certainly have provided Jung with the insight he needed to realize that he was not some kind of freak with a split personality, but merely a person who happened to be consciously aware of the presence of his own 'subjective mind', which in most people is merely a shadow glimpsed out of the corner of the eye. Instead, he dramatized Number 2 as the wise old man in eighteenth-century shoes, or as Goethe's Faust — and later still, as Nietzsche's Zarathustra. And this raised certain problems; for he was unable to admire Faust whole-heartedly — in fact, was inclined to feel him rather a fool — while he was rather repelled by Zarathustra's rhapsodic, biblical language, which struck him as overblown.

He also failed to recognize that Number 2 was the source of his dreams. Jung always attached tremendous importance to dreams, and it is not for nothing that his autobiography is called *Memories, Dreams, Reflections*; it probably contains more descriptions of dreams than any other autobiography. But from an early stage, he recognized clearly that his dreams were *saying* something to him. And one of his most important dreams occurred at this time. He was walking along at night, buffeted by wind and surrounded by whirling fog, holding in his hands a tiny light; he knew that everything depended on keeping this light alive. He looked behind him and saw that he was being followed by a gigantic black figure, which filled him with terror; yet he still recognized that he had to prevent the flame from being blown out. When he woke up, he realized that the black figure was his own shadow, a Spectre of the Brocken projected by the light he was carrying. 'I knew that this little light was my consciousness, the only light I have. My own understanding is the sole treasure I possess, and the greatest. Though infinitely small and fragile in comparison with the powers of darkness, it is still a light, my only light.' Ever since his experience of dispelling his fainting fits by an effort of will, Jung had recognized instinctively that the human mind is far more powerful than we suspect. This was the insight that finally caused the break with Freud, and developed into his own distinctive psychology.

Jung's father was becoming increasingly tense and irritable; in fact, he was nearing the end of his life, suffering from 'an illness that had no clear-cut medical basis'.* During his freshman year at the University of Basle, Jung was becoming increasingly aware that his father was a pathetic failure. He felt that 'the golden gates to . . . academic freedom were opening for me', they had once opened for his father. When his father came on a fraternity outing to a wine-growing village and delivered a humorous speech, Jung was aware that the spirit of his old student days was leaping up for a moment. He also realized that his father's life had come to a standstill after his graduation, and that it had since been a long anticlimax. Then why had it gone sour? He could find no answer. Soon afterwards, his father became bedridden; he died as Jung stood by the bed. His mother, who normally seemed to be a stolid and rather stupid woman, but who occasionally had flashes of a 'Number 2 personality', said in her Number 2 voice: 'He died in time for you.' Jung took this to mean that he was now at last free to choose his own path and to take on the responsibilities of an adult. In fact,

* Vincent Brome: *Jung*, p. 60.

he moved into his father's room, and doled out the housekeeping money to his mother, who was unable to manage the family's finances.

In spite of the university grant, Jung's student days were a time of endless poverty. He said later: 'I would not have missed this time of poverty. One learns to value simple things.'

He started to read Nietzsche, and found it intoxicating, particularly *Zarathustra*. But he came to recognize that Zarathustra was Nietzsche's Number 2 personality, and that Nietzsche had allowed it to become his dominant self. The result was the inflated language of *Zarathustra*, and Nietzsche's increasing manic self-assertiveness that ended in madness. (Jung was apparently unaware that Nietzsche's madness was due to syphilis.) He also read Edouard von Hartmann's remarkable — and now forgotten — work *The Philosophy of the Unconscious*, in which Hartmann argues that nature is driven by an immense unconscious will. Hartmann's 'unconscious' was not the unconscious mind that was even then — in the 1890s — being 'discovered' by Freud; but his hundreds of examples of instinctive behaviour in animals and birds must have given Jung an insight into the unconscious *yet purposive* realm of instinct. Jung was still a typical romantic, looking for something to give his life direction and purpose. And Hartmann and Nietzsche were piling fuel on the fires of intellectual rebellion.

But there was an even more important influence. In the library of the father of a classmate he came upon a small book about the beginnings of spiritualism. This had started in America in 1848, in the house of the Fox family in New York state, when strange rapping noises made them aware that the house was 'haunted'. The two Fox children, Kate and Margaret, established contact with the 'entity' through a code of raps, and were told that it was a pedlar who had been murdered in the house — human bones were later found buried in the cellar. In spite of the opposition of the Church, 'spiritualism' quickly spread across America, then to Europe. People who, like the Fox sisters, were able to go into a trance and establish contact with 'spirits' became known as 'mediums'. In France in the 1850s, an educationalist named Denizard Rivail discovered that two daughters of a friend were excellent mediums, and proceeded to address all kinds of questions to the 'spirits' about life after death and the meaning of human existence; he published his results, under the pseudonym Allen Kardec, in a work called *The Spirits' Book* in 1857; it became the 'Bible of spiritualism', and achieved immense influence. Spiritualism quickly became a religion. In the 1880s, a group of English philosophers, led by Henry Sidgwick and Frederic Myers, decided to set up a society for the scientific investigation of ghosts, poltergeists, telepathy and other manifestations of the paranormal; it became the Society for Psychical Research.

So by the time Jung discovered spiritualism, at the age of twenty-two, there was already a large body of serious work on psychical research, as well as innumerable volumes of unreliable anecdotes about ghosts and 'second sight'. Jung plunged into the subject and read everything he could find. Schoolfellows to whom he spoke about it were mostly either sceptical or uninterested. But it quickly became clear to Jung that when phenomena are reported from all over the world, over thousands of years, it is absurd to dismiss them as the result of fraud or imagination. 'I wondered at the sureness with which they could assert that things like ghosts and table turning were impossible and therefore fraudulent, and on the other hand, at the evidently anxious nature of their defensiveness. For myself I found such possibilities extremely interesting and attractive. They added another dimension to my life; the world gained depth and background.'

He recognized that these beliefs about spirits, precognition, animal clairvoyance, clocks that stopped at the time of someone's death, had been taken for granted by most country people during his childhood, and now his reading of serious works on psychic phenomena convinced him that such things could not be dismissed as superstitions. Yet the sophisticated urban world of Basle dismissed it all. It bolstered his self-esteem to see so clearly that the urban world was laughably narrow minded. But his intolerance and argumentativeness got him disliked, and aroused once again the old feelings of self-doubt and inferiority, which had to be fought and dismissed.

His scientific studies acted as a counterweight to the interest in occultism. He became a junior assistant in anatomy, then was placed in charge of a course in histology, the study of organic tissues. This was of immense importance for someone who needed success as badly as Jung did. He had turned into an obsessive worker; science became his most important form of relief. Once again, that experience of overcoming his fainting fits and plunging into study was proving to be the key to his self-development.

He was soon to experience an incursion of the occult into his personal life. Sitting one day at his textbooks, he heard a report like a pistol shot from the dining room next door, in which his mother was sitting. He rushed in, to find that the round walnut table had split from the rim to the centre. There was no obvious cause; it was a temperate day; the table had dried out over seventy years. Two weeks later, he came home to find his mother and sister in a state of agitation; there had been another loud report, but they could find no reason for it. Jung examined the sideboard, from which the sound had apparently come; inside, he found that the breadknife had snapped into several pieces. The next day Jung took the broken knife to a cutler to ask if he could think of any explanation; the cutler said it looked as if someone had deliberately broken the blade, a piece at a time, by sticking it into a crack.

A few weeks later, Jung heard that his cousin, Helly (Hélène) Preiswerk had developed mediumistic powers. Her grandfather, the Hebrew scholar the Revd Samuel Preiswerk, possessed these powers to such a degree that he lived in a household with two wives, one living and one dead. To the disgust of his second wife, the Revd Samuel would retire to his study once every week, and hold conversations with the spirit of his first wife, who sat in a chair specially reserved for her; this Noel Coward situation apparently went on for years. Other members of the family were also psychic; and, as we have seen, Jung regarded his mother as a dual personality, one of which possessed latent occult faculties.

In 1889, Helly Preiswerk was an unnattractive schoolgirl of 15, with a thin, pale face and a small compressed mouth; she was described by Jung as of 'mediocre intelligence, with no special gifts'. Helly had had an unhappy childhood; she was a member of a large family, and the children were ignored by their father and brutally treated by their mother. Her education was poor and she had little or no knowledge of literature.

In July 1899, she joined in experiments in 'table turning', which had the popularity of a parlour game; a group sit around a light table, their fingertips touching, and try to induce it to move. Under propitious circumstances, the table begins to vibrate, and may then slide around the floor, rise so only two legs are on the floor, and sometimes even float up into the air. At one of these sessions, Helly suddenly went very pale, closed her eyes, and went into a trance. She began to speak in a voice that was unlike her own, and in literary German instead of her usual Swiss dialect. When she recovered, she could remember nothing of what had happened, but had a severe headache.

Jung heard about these trance states in the following month, and began to attend the Sunday evening seances. By this time, Helly had a 'guide' or control, who claimed to be her grandfather, the Revd Samuel Preiswerk, and who was inclined to deliver unctuous religious discourses. A remarkable number of 'spirits' began to speak through Helly's mouth. One claimed to be the dead brother of a man who was present, and flirted outrageously with one of the ladies; others identified themselves as dead relatives of the medium. Then a man with a north German accent called Ulrich von Gerbenstein made his appearance. There was a girl who chatted swiftly in what sounded like a mixture of French and Italian, both languages being unknown to the medium. Finally, a spirit called Ivenes emerged, who claimed to be 'the real Hélène Preiswerk'. Ivenes claimed that she had once been Friederika Hauffe, the famous 'Seeress of Prevorst', about whom Justinus Kerner had written a celebrated book, a clergyman's wife who had been seduced by Goethe, a Saxon countess, a thirteenth-century French noblewoman who had been burnt as a witch, and a Christian martyr. What astonished Jung was that Ivenes seemed to be a mature and balanced woman, with considerable knowledge — far more knowledge than Helly could ever have acquired. Jung said that 'she could talk so seriously, so forcefully and convincingly that one almost had to ask oneself: Is this really a girl of fifteen and a half? One had the impression that a mature woman was being acted out with considerable dramatic talent.'

Helly claimed to spend every Wednesday night in the company of spirits, whom she saw clearly; she explained about 'star dwellers' who have no godlike souls but are far advanced in science, and described the canals and flying machines of Mars. She later developed a complex mystical system in which the forces of the universe are arranged symbolically in seven circles — when, years later, Jung stumbled upon the Mandala symbol, he concluded that Helly had dredged it up from the collective unconscious.

Over the course of the year 1899´900, the quality of the seances began to deteriorate as trivial spirits sometimes chattered for hours. Helly's powers were apparently fading. When, one day, she admitted to Jung that she had simulated trance, he lost interest in her. When he met her in Paris some years later, the subject of the seances was tactfully avoided. Helly became a dressmaker in Montpellier, and died at the age of thirty. After her death, Jung found himself speculating whether her unconscious mind knew that she was destined to die young, and whether the personality of Ivenes was some kind of compensation for this, an attempt to grow into the mature middle aged woman she would never become.

In 1902, in Zurich, Jung would produce his doctoral dissertation 'The Psychology and Pathology of So-called Occult Phenomena', which is mainly a detailed description of the case of Helly Preiswerk. By that time, Jung had reached the conclusion that Helly was a case of 'multiple personality' — a baffling and still only partly-understood phenomenon in which a number of persons seem to take over the same body (the 'three faces of Eve' case is perhaps the most famous in recent years). According to this theory, Helly was a kind of Walter Mitty whose compensatory fantasy life succeeded in bursting up from her unconscious mind, producing the various personalities. Thomson Jay Hudson, in *The Law of Psychic Phenomena*, had reached a similar conclusion about spiritualistic seances — that they are simply a manifestation of the incredible inventive and creative powers of the 'subjective mind'. Hudson had been present at a hypnotic session in which a young man was told that he was being introduced to Socrates; the young man looked profoundly impressed, and proceeded to hold a one-sided conversation with the spirit of the Greek philosopher. Requested by the hypnotist to repeat what Socrates was saying, he produced such a brilliant and complex system of philosophy that some people present were inclined to believe that he *was* actually talking to the ghost of Socrates.

Yet, as we have seen, Jung himself finally came to reject this wholly 'human' view of the paranormal and, tacitly at least, came to accept the existence of spirits. The 'psychological' view of spiritualism fails to cover the immensely complex range of phenomena. For example, in the famous 'Cross Correspondence' case, a number of mediums in different parts of the world all received 'messages' that purported to come from certain deceased founders of the Society for Psychical Research, messages that made sense only when put together, like a jigsaw puzzle. And Jung himself was a friend of a man, J. H. Hyslop, who had received convincing proof of survival, involving no less a person than William James. James and Hyslop promised one another that whoever died first would try to 'come back'. For years after James's death in 1910, nothing happened. Then a letter from Ireland told Hyslop that a 'spirit' called William James had communicated by means of a planchette, and asked them to contact a certain Professor Hyslop and ask him if he remembered some red pyjamas. Hyslop was baffled; it meant nothing to him. Then, in a flash, it came back: James and Hyslop had been on a European holiday as young men, and had arrived in Paris late one night to find that their luggage had not yet arrived. Hyslop went out to buy pyjamas, and could only find a lurid red pair; for days, James teased Hyslop about his poor taste in pyjamas. But Hyslop had long ago forgotten about the incident.

It would be hard to think of a more convincing proof of 'survival'. And in view of Jung's first-hand knowledge of the case, it is hard to understand how he could ever have swallowed the 'psychological' view of psychic phenomena. The uncharitable view would be that it was simply intellectual dishonesty, the 'double-think' that is characteristic of so many scientists who are anxious to be regarded as 'tough minded' (an expression coined by William James). But we should also bear in mind that Helly Preiswerk was Jung's cousin, and that Jung quickly came to recognize that she thoroughly enjoyed the attention she received as a result of her trances. Helly was not a famous medium — just a girl Jung had known since she was a child. It was inevitable that Jung should allow familiarity to breed a certain contempt — revealed in his comment that she was 'of mediocre intelligence, with no special gifts'. Moreover, she finally admitted cheating in a later seance. It was natural that a young doctor should be inclined to take a 'reductionist' view of her case.

But when, not long after this, he came upon Krafft-Ebing's *Textbook of Psychiatry*, with its remark about 'diseases of the personality', his memory of the seances must have played its part in the excitement that overwhelmed him. The psychiatric lectures included in his medical course had bored him because most doctors then regarded mental illness as physical in origin — due to deterioration of brain tissue, or disease of the nervous system. Krafft-Ebing was suggesting that the answer should be sought in the realm of the human soul — the 'psyche'. The result must have been like the sudden opening of a door. 'These few hints cast such a transfiguring light on psychiatry that I was irretrievably drawn under its spell.' He was like an explorer who has suddenly obtained proof of the real existence of Atlantis or King Solomon's mines.

'The decision was taken. When I informed my teacher in internal medicine of my intention, I could read in his face his amazement and disappointment. My old wound, the feeling of being an outsider and of alienating others, began to ache again.' But with this path to discovery that had now opened up, he no longer cared about being an outsider. At last he had a direction.

Two

How to Become a Scientist

It was Jung's good fortune to be accepted by Eugen Bleuler, one of the foremost psychiatrists in Europe, as an assistant at the Burghölzli Mental Hospital in Zurich. Bleuler — who is responsible for inventing the term schizophrenia — had himself been the director of the Burghölzli for only two years when Jung arrived in December 1900. Before that he had been in charge of a lunatic asylum at Rheinau, full of old, demented patients who were regarded as incurable vegetables. Bleuler had accepted this as a challenge, and set out determinedly to get to know every one of them personally and to try and get to the root of their problems. Instead of treating their delusions as incomprehensible nonsense, he tried to understand precisely how they had come about. It might be said that Bleuler treated their delusions as a literary critic treats a novel — as a *creation* that can be understood. And in an age that regarded mental illness as physical in origin — a view known as organicism — this was a tremendous step forward. He was brilliantly successful.

Jung described the Burghölzli as a kind of monastery. Bleuler expected from his staff the same fanatical devotion that he brought to his work. But he was no authoritarian — his attitude was more like that of a kindly elder brother. Jung was embarrassed, when he arrived, that Bleuler insisted on carrying his case up to his room.

Alcohol was not permitted; food was plentiful but plain. Jung had to rise at 6.30 and make his rounds before a general staff meeting at 8.30. The hospital doors were closed at 10 p.m., and only senior residents were allowed keys.

But it was precisely what Jung needed. He had at last found something that could absorb his total enthusiasm. For him, the mental world of the patients was an endless series of fascinating puzzles. His dedication was so much greater than that of of most of his colleagues that he felt an understandable sense of superiority. After about a week he began spending most of his time alone, and within six months had read the fifty volumes of the *Journal of Psychiatry (Allgemeine Zeitschrift für Psychiatrie)* from beginning to end. Being surrounded by mental illness seems to have aroused the kind of morbid enthusiasm that a child feels for violence. 'I wanted to know how the human mind reacted to the sight of its own destruction, for psychiatry seemed to me an articulate expression of that biological reaction which seizes upon the so-called healthy mind in the presence of mental illness.'

Writing about this period later, Jung showed a curious lack of generosity towards Bleuler. He states that what dominated his interest was the question: 'What actually takes place inside the mentally ill?', and then adds the incredible statement: 'nor had any of my colleagues concerned themselves with such problems'. Since this was the very essence of Bleuler's contribution, such a remark seems incomprehensible. Neither does Jung acknowledge his own indebtedness to Bleuler. The explanation is probably that Jung's fascination with the mysteries of mental illness was equal to Bleuler's own, and he did not need Bleuler's example to encourage it; so he regarded Bleuler with the unconscious jealousy of a man who feels that someone else has anticipated his own discovery. What seems clear is that Jung threw himself into the work of the hospital with a dedication equal to Bleuler's own.

Bleuler suspected that illnesses like schizophrenia (loss of contact with reality) may be due partly to some physical cause, such as hormone deficiency. (And the latest discoveries suggest that he may well be right.) But his real contribution was to recognize that illness is basically a question of the patient's own *will*, or lack of it. In that case, the main problem was to stimulate the patient into using his will, instead of remaining a leaden, passive weight. He might, for example, discharge a severely ill patient back into home life — rather in the spirit of teaching someone to swim by throwing him into the swimming pool. He was also a pioneer of 'work therapy'.

Jung gives an example of the kind of case that fascinated him. One of his female patients was suffering from acute depression. By studying her dreams, and subjecting her to 'word association tests' — one of Jung's major innovations at the Burghölzli — he uncovered a story of guilt that explained her illness. She had been in love with the son of a wealthy industrialist; but since he seemed indifferent to her, she married another man. Five years later, an old friend told her that the man *had* been in love with her, and had been upset when she married. She began to feel depressed. One day, when bathing her children, she noticed that her baby daughter was sucking water from the sponge — tainted river water; her depression made her indifferent. In fact, she also allowed her small son to drink river water. The girl died, but the son was unaffected. The girl was her favourite, and it was soon after this that her depression reached a point at which it looked like schizophrenia, and she was hospitalized.

Having discovered his patient's secret, Jung was confronted with the problem of what to do. He made the decision to tell her. It proved to be the right one. Knowing that someone shared her secret was like confession; within two weeks, she was well enough to be discharged, and was never again hospitalized.

It was, of course, an extremely risky decision to take, and Bleuler, with his deep concern for the patient, might well not have taken it. In reading Jung's account of his cases, it is impossible not to be aware that his success was due partly to an element of ruthlessness; he was dominated by curiosity rather than compassion. This same ruthlessness can be seen in a later case, involving the governor of the Bank of England, Sir Montagu Norman, who began suffering from manic-depression which, in its manic phase, amounted to delusions of grandeur. Delusions of grandeur are sometimes associated with syphilis and general paralysis of the insane. Jung ordered a blood test, and informed Norman that he was syphilitic. Norman's brother Ronald heard the verdict from his shattered brother and rushed to see Jung, who firmly repeated his verdict, and stated that Norman would be dead within months. In fact, the blood test proved to be mistaken, and Norman was treated by another doctor for manic-depression and partly cured. Jung's own superabundant vitality seems to have blunted the fine edge of human sympathy that is necessary to be a good psychiatrist.

What was exciting Jung so much, in these early days, was his recognition that mental illness has its root in the unconscious mind, not in some deterioration in the brain or nervous system. It could therefore be reduced to a simple problem: how to 'get into' the unconscious and find out what is going on there. At that time, the most useful method was the word association test invented by Sir Francis Galton and refined by Wundt. When it was discovered that reaction time was longer when the word had unpleasant associations, the psychiatrist suddenly had a clue to the patient's repressions.

Now one of Bleuler's most important insights was that schizophrenia involved a loosening of the patient's mental associations. Consciousness, after all, is a matter of associations. If a cow looks at an umbrella, it means nothing to it because an umbrella has no associations for a cow; for a human being it has dozens. Our minds are a *web of associations*. When a person 'lets go', like the mother who let her child suck dirty water, it is the associations that are being let go of. So when Bleuler recognized that the word association test can provide a key to mental illness, he had taken a practical step to understanding the 'geography of consciousness'.

Jung had already invented his own mental stethoscope for sounding out the unconscious: dream analysis. Ever since he was a child, he had been fascinated by his own dreams, feeling instinctively that they were trying to 'tell' him something. Now, using dream analysis in conjunction with the word association test, he realized that he had the key to many mysteries of the mind. He had become, so to speak, a psychiatric Sherlock Holmes. Sometimes, even his own dreams helped him to solve a case. He was consulted by a pretty young Jewess with a severe anxiety neurosis. On the previous night, he had dreamed of a young girl whose problem was a father fixation. As the young Jewess talked to him, and he had to admit that he was unable to gain any insight into her problem, he suddenly thought: 'She is the girl of my dream.' He could detect no sign of a father complex, but when he asked her about her grandfather, she closed her eyes for a moment, and Jung inferred that this was the root of the problem. Her grandfather had been a rabbi, a kind of saint who was also reputed to possess second sight. Her father turned his back on all this and abandoned the Jewish faith. Jung suddenly told the girl 'You have your neurosis because the fear of God has got into you.' Later, he dreamed that he was kneeling, and presenting the girl with an umbrella, as if she was a goddess. When he told her this dream, her neurosis quickly vanished.

A case like this makes the reader suspect that Jung was madder than his patient, and such a reaction is not entirely unwarranted. To begin with, Jung assumes that his first dream was telling him something about a patient he saw for the first time the next day. Next, he assumes that the grandfather is somehow the key to her neurosis. Finally, he concludes that the girl has the makings of a saint, but is somehow trapped in her own picture of herself as a pretty, superficial creature with nothing in her head but flirtations and clothes. What Jung is doing is to use his own completely irrational reactions to provide insight into a problem that defied his conscious intellect. It is conceivable that he may have been quite wrong about the cause of her neurosis, and his feeling that she had the making of a saint. But his instinct made him treat her as someone who deserved to be treated as a goddess, not as a silly little girl, and this had the effect of boosting her self-esteem and curing the problem. We must also take into account the analyst himself. Jung was a massively built, handsome young man with a commanding perso- nality, and the sheer force of his presence — and his implied admiration — must have acted upon the girl's ego like a soothing balm. So whether or not Jung was correct about her, he had intuitively hit upon the right method of galvanizing her self-respect and her vital forces.

The case should also make us somewhat cautious about Jung's whole approach to psychiatry. He wanted to treat it as an exact science, which meant finding scientific justi- fications for the things he did instinctively. His paper 'On So-called Occult Phenomena', about his cousin Helly, is an example: Helly has to be rammed into a mould that fits — in this case, multiple personality. But as we read the case, we become aware that her mediumship was far more complicated than the Walter Mitty fantasy to which Jung tries to reduce it, just as Sir Montagu Norman's case was more complicated than syphilis. In those early days, Jung was obsessed with sounding like a paid-up member of the scientific establishment, and the result is a kind of rigidity in his mental categories, a lack of perceptiveness.

It is tempting to regard his association with Pierre Janet in the winter of 1902-3 as another example of the lack of perceptiveness. Jung obtained leave of absence to spend the winter in Paris, studying under Janet, who was at the time fifty-three years old. Janet had caused a sensation in 1885 with a paper about a patient called Leonie, an exceptionally good hypnotic subject, and a remarkable case of multiple personality.* Janet could place Leonie in a state of hypnosis when she was on the other side of Le Havre, and summon her to come to his house. Such a discovery should have revolutionized psychology; but it was a little too startling to be absorbed, even by Jung.

In 1902, when Jung came to Paris, Janet had developed a simple and comprehensive theory of the cause of mental illness. Like Bleuler, Janet recognized that an illness like schizophrenia is a *scattering* of attention, a loss of concentration; we express it precisely when we say that someone is 'not all there'. All where? All *there*, where the mind should be focused. Focusing, concentration, is a mental act, and it is a function of the will just as breathing is a function of the lungs or digestion of the stomach. The definition of a healthy person is a person who is focusing and concentrating with a sense of vital purpose.

Janet described this act of focusing as 'psychological tension'. Psychological tension is the deliberate *ordering* of our 'psychological force' — our energies.

If I face some prospect with a groan of boredom, it produces a feeling that could be translated: 'Oh *no*!', and a loss of 'psychological tension'; my energy seems to spread out, like a glass of water knocked over a table top. Conversely, the moment I become deeply interested in something, I increase my psychological tension, and the result is a sudden feeling of increased energy and vitality — psychological force.

So in an important sense, I am in charge of my own vitality. I merely have to think to myself 'How fascinating', and *concentrate*, to experience an instant rise in my vital tension.

But if I can command my own vitality, then what causes

* See my *Mysteries*, p. 209.

neurosis? It is a simple mechanism. When I have *allowed* the loss of psychological tension to develop, out of laziness or boredom or a sense of defeat, molehills turn into mountains, and suddenly the real enemy is not the world 'out there', but my own negative forces — mistrust, self-pity, self-doubt. I am like the Balinese dancer in the Danny Kaye film who manages to tie himself in knots. It is the vicious-circle effect.

What can rescue us from this vicious circle of defeat and weakness? Any sudden challenge or stimulus that touches our *sense of reality*. Neurosis is essentially a loss of contact with reality. We all possess a 'reality function' — the ability to reach out and make contact with reality. It is obviously weaker in children than adults, because the child has had less experience of reality, and therefore finds it harder to evoke reality 'inside his own head', so to speak. For this is what is at issue: the ability to *summon* reality, like summoning the genie from the lamp, and to make it present itself inside one's own head. This explains why we all hunger for experience, and hate inactivity; we want to strengthen our 'reality function'.

So what Janet is saying is that we *can* strengthen our reality function, and pull ourselves out of that sticky swamp of subjectivity. When that happens, the process is reversed. Mountains turn into molehills as I realize that all problems can be solved provided I increase my psychological tension: a kind of optimistic determination. Neurosis could be compared to a sleeper who is tangled in the blankets and has a nightmare that he is in the grip of a boa constrictor. The moment he wakes up, he sighs with relief to realize that the situation was not nearly as serious as he thought. He only felt helpless because he was asleep. Now he is awake, his *free will* can operate. And as he summons psychological tension — that sense of optimistic determination — he realizes that he is also summoning the energy necessary to put his purposes into operation: psychological force.

In short, Janet's psychology is fundamentally optimistic and non-mechanistic. And since Jung himself was full of optimism and enthusiasm in that winter of 1902, it might seem reasonable to expect that he would recognize Janet as a kindred spirit. Why did he not do so? Perhaps *because* Janet's ideas are so sane and optimistic. Jung was only just emerging from the dark world of German romanticism, of Faust and Schopenhauer and Nietzsche, and he was busy counterbalancing this aspect of his personality with precise experiment that deepened his own 'reality function'. Temperamentally speaking, he was out of sympathy with Janet's Gallic logic and clarity.

Besides, during that first Paris trip, Jung's head was filled with other things besides the psychology of neurosis. He was in love with an attractive girl who was seven years his junior, and who had just agreed to marry him. Jung says that he first saw Emma Rauschenbach, the daughter of a wealthy industrialist, when he was twenty-one and she was fourteen; she was standing at the top of a flight of stairs in a Zurich hotel, and Jung turned to his companion and said: 'That girl will be my wife.' Jung's love letters are still unpublished, so we lack details of the progress of the romance; but we know he accompanied her on picnics, and took her for walks by the lake. The first time he proposed to her, she turned him down, which must have been a shock to his own healthily developed ego. But by the time he left for Paris, she had accepted him, and it was probably this that was partly responsible for the 'mild state of intoxication' that he experienced all winter. He does not seem to have been a particularly assiduous student — Janet, in any case, only lectured once a week — and spent a great deal of time wandering around and looking at the sights. Money was still short and he often dined off a bag of roast chestnuts.

Then, back in Zurich, a new life began. In February 1903 he married Emma. They went on honeymoon to Lake Como. A flat was provided for the couple in the Burghölzli, immediately above Bleuler's flat. Suddenly, life was delightful: meals in his own home, enough money to entertain friends, shopping expeditions with Emma. Everyone liked her and thought Jung had made an excellent choice; to Jung, accustomed to poverty, the marriage must have seemed a foretaste of success.

Jung was obsessed with work. There were more word association tests, and tests with a galvonometer attached to the skin, constituting a kind of lie detector; his papers on these subjects form a large volume of the Collected Works. But luck was also on his side. One day, a 58-year-old woman came on crutches to one of Jung's lectures; she was suffering from paralysis of the left leg. She began to talk about her symptoms, and Jung prepared to use her to demonstrate hypnosis to his students. To his astonishment, she went into a trance as soon as he said 'I am going to hypnotize you.' And as Jung stood there, feeling rather uncomfortable, she talked volubly about her dreams. After half an hour, he tried to wake her; he only succeeded after ten minutes. As she looked around in confusion, Jung said: 'I am the doctor and everything is all right!' 'But I am cured!' cried the woman, and threw away her crutches. Jung turned to his students and said triumphantly: 'Now you see what can be done with hypnosis!'

When his next course of lectures began the following summer, the woman reappeared, complaining of violent pains in her back. Questioning elicited the fact that the pains had started immediately after she read about Jung's lecture in a newspaper. The same story repeated itself; she fell into a trance spontaneously, and woke up cured.

The woman went around Zurich talking about Jung's 'miracle cure', and it was because of this that he began to receive his first private patients. Further investigation of the woman's life uncovered the reasons behind the miraculous cure. She had a feeble-minded son who had a minor job in Jung's department in the hospital. She had dreamed about the future success of her only child; his mental illness was a terrible blow. So, in effect, she had transferred her hopes and expectations to Jung; she saw him as her 'son'.

Jung decided to explain all this to the woman. 'She took it very well, and did not again suffer a relapse.' So by explaining the cause of her problem to her, he had solved the problem. By personal experience, Jung had confirmed one of the central ideas of his controversial Viennese colleague, Sigmund Freud: that the cure of neurosis consists in dragging it into the light of consciousness.

In fact, Jung had become increasingly interested in Freud since he re-read *The Interpretation of Dreams* soon after his marriage. He had read it for the first time in 1900, before he came to the Burghölzli, having always been deeply interested in dreams. At that time, he had found it unimpressive. Freud's dream analyses often seemed absurdly far-fetched. For example, one patient related to him a dream in which her husband had suggested that the piano ought to be tuned, and she had replied: 'It's not worth while', and referred to the piano as a 'disgusting box'. Further questioning revealed that the phrase 'It isn't worth while' had been used by the patient on the previous day, when she called on a woman friend who asked her to take off her coat; she had said: 'It isn't worth while — I can only stay a moment.' Freud recalled that on the previous day, during analysis, the woman had taken hold of her coat where a button had come undone. He jumped to the conclusion that she was saying, in effect: 'Don't bother to look in — it isn't worth while.' In her dream, her 'chest', revealed by the open coat, became a 'box'.

It is possible to see why Jung was not impressed by his first reading of *The Interpretation of Dreams*. But his clinical experience had convinced him that 'repression' plays an important part in mental illness, just as Freud had said. Janet had said that hysteria was due basically to a kind of enfeeblement of the will, which led to the 'splitting of consciousness'. Freud had contradicted Janet, arguing that hysteria was due to the repression of some unpleasant experience or idea — as in the case of Jung's patient who had 'unconsciously' poisoned her daughter with polluted water. Moreover, Jung had had his own early experience of the effect of repression — when, as a schoolboy, he had repressed the thought of a turd falling from God's throne on to the cathedral roof. So a second reading of *The Interpretation of Dreams* filled him with admiration for Freud's clinical insights.

His chief misgiving lay in Freud's insistence that *all* repressions are associated with sex. This was clearly untrue; the falling turd had nothing to do with sex — it was a question of blasphemy — and the woman's 'poisoning' of her daughter was a social rather than a sexual matter. 'From my practice, I was familiar with numerous cases of neurosis in which the question of sexuality played a subordinate part.' But this small area of disagreement seemed trivial compared to the increasingly large areas of agreement — Jung was at the time unaware of how passionately Freud felt about his sexual theory of neurosis. Jung was now putting together his second major publication, *The Psychology of Dementia Praecox* (the first was his *Studies in Word Association*, which appeared in 1906), and Freudian notions were playing an increasingly important part in his outlook. Dementia praecox — for which, in 1909, Bleuler invented the term schizophrenia — meant dissociation from reality, as in catatonia, where the patient stares blankly into space; it was originally thought to be a purely organic disorder, due to brain deterioration. In any case, it tended to be dismissed simply as madness, in which the patient's delusions were arbitrary and unexplainable. Jung's word association tests convinced him that this was not so: that, like hysteria, schizophrenia was due to repressions. He reached another intresting conclusion: that in schizophrenia, the ego has split up into several sub-egos, or 'complexes'. (Jung was responsible for introducing the term 'complex' in this sense.) In effect, the patient became several people — an insight that Jung had originally developed in his paper on his cousin Helly.

It could be said that there was no genuine disagreement between Jung and Janet. Janet had said that schizophrenia is 'dissociation', a certain *spreading apart* of consciousness, like a raft whose ropes have begun to break, so it drifts apart. Jung himself accepted this view. But his own experience of fainting fits at the age of twelve had made him aware that there is more to it than this. The insight aided him in treating a female patient in 1906; the woman suffered from a constant feeling of exhaustion, and from hysterical hallucinations. Jung wrote: 'The twitching in the arm conveniently began, which then ultimately served the purpose of making it completely impossible to go to school. The patient now also admits that she could have suppressed the twitching then if she had tried. *But it suited her to be ill.'* So Jung had added an important insight to Janet's concept of mental illness — an element that Janet himself (when Jung spoke to him about it in 1907) was inclined to underestimate.

So in 1906, Jung could have been said to be poised between Freudianism and 'Janet-ism'. He was cautious about being too open in his support of Freud, for Freud's insistence that all neurosis is sexual aroused a mixture of fury and derision among professional psychologists, and Jung had no desire to be tarred with the same brush. Besides, Jung felt — quite rightly — that he had discovered the repressive element in neurosis for himself — through his word association tests — without any help from Freud.

And at this point, Jung's Protestant morality inter-
vened. In writing up his association experiments, he was
tempted to leave out all mention of Freud. In the case of
the patient with the twitching arm, it was clear to Jung at a
fairly early stage that 'she is trying to gratify her desire for
love by falling in love with the doctor' — what Freud
called the 'transference phenomenon'. He also concluded
that her problem was basically due to sexual repression.
But it was he, Jung, who had seen this, without help from
Freud. 'Once, while I was in my laboratory and reflecing
again upon these questions, the devil whispered to me
that I would be justified in publishing the results of my
experiments and my conclusions without mentioning
Freud . . . But then I heard the voice of my second
personality: "If you do a thing like that . . . it would be a
piece of trickery. You cannot build your life upon a lie."'
And from then on, says Jung, 'I became an open partisan
of Freud's, and fought for him.'

The result was that Jung wrote to Freud, sending him a
copy of his *Diagnostic Association Studies* — the word
association book. He must have been flattered to receive,
on 11 April 1906, a letter from Freud declaring that he had
already hurried out and bought the book before he heard
from Jung. The letter finished: 'I am confident that you
will often be in a position to back me up, but I shall also
gladly accept correction.' That sounded promising. It
would be some time before Jung discovered that the one
point on which Freud would never accept correction
would be the one on which Jung most passionately
disagreed with him.

Jung's letter was a great event in Freud's life. What Jung
had probably not realized when he wrote to Freud was
that Freud felt himself to be totally alone and without
support. At the age of fifty, Freud still felt that he might
succumb to ridicule and hostility, and vanish into obscurity. This support from a respectable 'academic' psychologist arrived like manna from heaven. And when Freud
learned that Jung had persuaded Bleuler and other
colleagues that Freud's views deserved serious consideration, he could probably hardly believe his luck. It looked
like a sudden and complete breakthrough.

A few weeks later, at a conference at Baden-Baden, Jung
had a chance to display his public adherence to Freudian-

ism. A certain Professor Gustav Aschaffenburg attacked pschoanalysis as objectionable and immoral, and another professor described it as evil. And here Jung was made to recognize the central problem involved in his new allegiance. For the attacks were on Freud's insistence that neurosis springs *entirely* from sexual problems, and Jung agreed with them. In his reply, he referred to Aschaffenburg's 'very moderate and cautious criticism', and pointed out that Aschaffenburg had left most of Freud's theory — on dreams, jokes and disturbances of everyday thinking — untouched. Ernest Jones, Freud's biographer, felt that Jung's reply was ineffective; but it was probably as effective as Jung wanted it to be.

The correspondence between Freud and Jung grew warmer. Jung sent Freud his book on dementia praecox, with an apologetic letter for not giving him more generous acknowledgement. 'I understand perfectly that you cannot be anything but dissatisfied with my book since it treats your researches too ruthlessly.' But, he explains, he has to worry about the reactions of the great German public, which means that he has to preserve 'a certain reserve and the hint of an independent judgement regarding your researches'. There is a hint of Machiavellianism here in the suggestion that he does not, in fact, have any such reservations. The truth was that Jung was closer to Aschaffenburg's position than to Freud's.

But Freud was not disposed to quarrel. He wrote back a flattering letter about Jung's book. In March 1907, the two men finally met in Vienna. It was something like love at first sight. This is not too strong a description. Freud undoubtedly had a touch of homosexuality in his composition — it shows in close relations with friends like Fliess — and Jung's biographer Vincent Brome suggests that Jung was aware of a streak of homosexuality in his own makeup. With Emma present, Jung talked solidly for three hours, and Freud seems to have been content to listen. Then Freud took over the conversation, neatly grouped Jung's basic points under a number of headings, and proceeded to discuss these. They talked on, with short breaks, for thirteen hours.

Freud was determined that the meeting should be a success. Jung was his passport to academic respectability and acceptance. This massive, broad-shouldered man, with his blue eyes, close-cropped hair and military bearing (he was, like all Swiss, in the auxiliary army) was an overwhelming experience; Freud was swept away by his intelligence as well as by his wide knowledge. The Freud family was perhaps a little less impressed; they observed only that he ignored them as he talked in an endless flow. But for Freud and Jung, the meeting was an enormous success. Freud seems to have had no reservations; he began to think immediately about Jung as his closest associate and his successor. He wrote to Jung a few days after the meeting that he could 'hope for no one better than yourself . . . to continue and complete my work'. His attitude was not unlike that of a man who has become engaged to be married.

It was Jung who, after the meeting, seems to have begun to wonder whether the marriage was really desirable. The basic fact remained that he simply could not agree with Freud that sex is the basis of *all* neurosis. And although their discussion had apparently been wide-ranging and completely free, without real disagreements, it struck him later that when the subject of sex came into the conversation, Freud ceased to sound detached and critical, and talked with the passion of a religious convert.

Why *was* Freud so obsessed with his sexual theory? The question is as difficult to answer now as it was then, in the days when most doctors regarded it as a form of mild insanity. After Freud's rise to world fame — some twenty years after his meeting with Jung — there was a general agreement that the answer to that question was: Because it is true. But in the years since Freud's death, there has been a slow swing back towards the original view: that Freud simply went too far in his emphasis on 'the sexual theory'. And the question of why Freud regarded it as a kind of religion remains as puzzling and insistent as ever.

There is, of course, no difficulty in understanding the steps that led Freud to the sexual theory. The first had been the famous case of 'Anna O-', in fact a Jewish girl named Bertha Pappenheim. Bertha had gone into depression after witnessing the death — after a long and painful illness — of her father. She would fall into trance-like states, in which she muttered strange phrases and did irrational things. She was being treated by Freud's close colleague and mentor, Josef Breuer, and seems to have fallen in love with him. One day, she fell into a state of hysteria and Breuer was called to see her. He was shocked to observe her lying on the bed and jerking her hips up and down as if having sexual intercourse. Breuer left Vienna hastily with his wife the following day. Freud was greatly struck by the case.

Four years later, in 1885, Freud went to Paris to study under the famous Professor Charcot at the Salpêtrière hospital, and overheard a doctor saying that what a certain hysterical woman needed was 'repeated doses of a normal penis'. Again, he pondered. The period with Charcot brought another insight. Charcot used to give public demonstrations of hypnosis, often with spectacular effects — such as making the patient bark like a dog or flap his arms like a bird. Freud observed such baffling phenomena as hysterical pregnancy, in which a woman's stomach swelled up as if she was really pregnant, and hysterical paralysis, in which a patient might lose the use of arms or legs. He also took to heart Charcot's remark that hypnosis and hysteria are closely related — in fact, the hypnosis *is* a form of hysteria. A patient under hypnosis could be told that he would be paralysed when he woke up, and he *would* be paralysed; he could be told that the hypnotist had touched him with a red hot iron — when it was merely a finger — and a blister would develop. Clearly, there is a part of the mind that is far more powerful than the conscious ego, and which can cause these astonishing effects. Freud was the first doctor to grasp the immense power of the unconscious, and it is his chief title to fame. Before Freud, the 'unconscious' had merely meant instinct, or mechanical reactions. It was Freud who created a new picture of the mind as a kind of sea, with a few feet of sunlit upper waters — called consciousness — and vast black depths, full of strange monsters. This vision transformed psychology, virtually creating a new science, to be known as 'depth psychology'.

Soon after his return from Paris, Freud was slightly shaken when a female patient flung her arms around his neck — they were interrupted by the entry of a servant. To Freud, the episode was revelatory; it revealed to him that the cure of a patient might depend on her falling in love with the doctor — the phenomenon he labelled 'transference'. He began to question other patients about their sex lives, which led some of them to turn their backs on him. But a surprisingly large number of women admitted that they had been assaulted or seduced by their fathers. For a while, Freud actually held the astonishing view that the majority of neuroses are caused by childhood seductions — an indication of his increasing obsession with sexual problems. It took him about ten years to recognize that most of these accounts of childhood rapes were fantasies, produced by the patient in response to Freud's own obvious promptings. Yet this did not convince him that his sexual theory was mistaken. On the contrary, it seemed to him to reveal that the women really had a secret wish to be seduced by their fathers — otherwise, why should they lie about it? He developed the theory of the Oedipus complex: that the son has a desire to sleep with his mother, and therefore to kill his father — his chief rival, who in turn would secretly wish to kill the son, or at least castrate him. It was at this point that Josef Breuer, Freud's closest colleague, felt that it was time to protest: surely this was going a little too far? Angrily, Freud broke with Breuer.

The Oedipus complex theory undoubtedly had some personal basis. When Freud was born, in 1856, his mother was a pretty vivacious girl of twenty-one; his father was forty-one. A picture of Freud, aged sixteen, with his mother still shows her as attractive and desirable. His father was by then fifty-seven. It seems perfectly conceivable that Freud desired his mother sexually and indulged in erotic fantasies about her. If this seems unlikely for a well-brought-up Jewish boy in the the Victorian era, it is worth recalling that one of his chief disciples, Wilhelm Reich, entertained similar feelings about his own mother. When Reich was thirteen, he realized that his mother was having a sexual affair with his tutor. A recent biography of Reich (by Myron Sharaf) reveals that Reich's first reaction was to wonder if he could use his knowledge to blackmail his mother into having sex with him. (In fact, he informed his father, and his mother committed suicide.)

If Freud entertained similar fantasies about his own mother, it would certainly explain his peculiar, obsessive attitude towards the sexual theory. Vienna in the 1870s was as full of morbid sexual repressions as Victorian

London; the very idea of incest would have been shockingly unmentionable. But Bertha Pappenheim's romantic interest in Josef Breuer, a man old enough to be her father, carried a suggestion of incest; so did a dream that she had when sitting by her dying father's bedside — of a black snake wriggling on to the bed. (Freud, of course, saw the snake as a penis symbol.) Freud was obviously both shocked and fascinated by the confessions of his female patients that they had been seduced by their fathers — so much so that he leapt to the preposterous conclusion that this was a common cause of neurosis. This suggests a man in whom the incest theme touched very deep emotional springs; and it is hard to see why this should be so unless he himself had fantasized — actively and for a long period — about having sexual intercourse with his mother.

When Jung raises Freud's sexual obsession in his autobiography, he carefully steers clear of this notion. 'Freud never asked himself why he was compelled to talk continually of sex, why this idea had taken such possession of him. He remained unaware that his "monotony of interpretation" expressed a flight from himself, or from that other side of him that might perhaps be called mystical . . . ' Which is, of course, begging the question: for the problem is *why* Freud should want to flee from himself. But where Freud's father is concerned, Jung is willing to be more open. He describes how, when he and Freud were on their way to America in 1909, Freud suddenly fainted as Jung talked about the peat bog corpses found in Northern Germany. Afterwards, Freud accused Jung of talking about corpses because he had death wishes towards him. Jung says that he was alarmed by the intensity of Freud's fantasies. Again in 1912, when Jung was discussing the Pharaoh Ikhnaton at a congress, and contradicting the notion that Ikhnaton had removed his father's name from inscriptions because he hated him, Freud slid off his chair in a faint. Jung points out that 'the fantasy of father-murder was common to both cases'. But why should Freud have fainted when Jung *denied* that Ikhnaton hated his father? Jung's comment about the strength of Freud's fantasies provides the answer. Jung clearly suspected that Freud *had* fantasized about murdering his father and seducing his mother, and that Jung's denial of Ikhnaton's patricidal tendencies aroused in

Freud an intense feeling of guilt, the kind of feeling that may make a teenager blush when someone discusses masturbation.

Jung prefers to gloss over the obvious truth that the real difference between himself and Freud is that his own mother was fat and ugly, so there was no temptation to dream of seducing her, and that his father was pathetic and unsuccessful, so there was no temptation to fantasize about killing him.

Jung was in a difficult position. Freud was an extremely powerful personality, who knew all there was to know about inspiring loyalty, trust, affection, even pity. Jung could say later: 'I see him as a tragic figure; for he was a great man, and what is more, a man in the grip of his daimon.' But in 1908, Jung was also in the grip of Freud's daimon, his tremendous charisma. Freud's aim was to bend Jung to his will, to cajole and persuade and seduce him into dropping his reservations, and to become the leading exponent of the sexual theory, Freud's spiritual heir. Jung's letters to Freud all begin 'Dear Professor Freud'. Freud's to Jung begin 'Dear Friend'. Freud was offering his own affection and loyalty in exchange for Jung's. But there could be no final argument about the sexual theory: that was not negotiable.

What Freud failed to realize was that Jung found the sexual theory, in the last analysis, slightly repellent. Freud was taken in by Jung's air of efficiency, the steel-rimmed spectacles, the enthusiasm for experiment. But Jung was not fundamentally a scientist; he was a romantic, a man whose deepest feelings had been aroused in the past by Goethe and Schopenhauer and Nietzsche, not by Galton and Wundt and Krafft-Ebing. Jung had turned to science to strengthen his 'reality function', to create a personality capable of meeting the world on its own terms. But there was still a part of him that longed for the 'horns of elfland'. Freud's sexual obsession was an affront to the poet in him. His real feelings emerged in two dreams. In one he saw a sour-looking old customs official who was, in fact, a ghost. It was a customs official's job to examine suitcases for contraband — contraband ideas as well as goods. 'I could not refuse to see the analogy with Freud.' In the other dream he was in a modern city when he saw a knight in full armour, wearing a white tunic with a red cross — a crusader; no one else seemed to notice him. Jung associated the knight with his own quest for the 'grail', for some deeper meaning in existence; it was a symbol of his own essential self.

It was therefore impossible that Jung should finally capitulate to the sexual theory; it would have been spiritual suicide. As it was, he was profoundly repelled by Freud's dogmatic materialism. 'Whenever, in a person or in a work of art, an expression of spirituality (in the intellectual, not the supernatural sense) came to light, he suspected it, and insinuated that it was repressed sexuality. Anything that could not be interpreted as sexuality he referred to as "psychosexuality". I protested that this hypothesis, carried to its logical conclusion, would lead to an annihilating judgement upon culture. Culture would then appear as a mere farce, the morbid consequence of repressed sexuality. "Yes", he assented, "so it is, and that is just a curse of fate against which we are powerless to contend". I was by no means disposed to agree . . . but I still did not feel competent to argue it out with him.'

But he argued it out with himself. The result was the slow emergence of his own alternative to the sexual theory.

Three

How to Lose Friends and Alienate People

By 1909, at the age of 33, Jung was becoming as well known in Zurich as Freud in Vienna — largely due to his efforts on Freud's behalf.

Unfortunately, he lacked the peace of mind to enjoy his increasing celebrity. Writing, lecturing, treating patients and organizing a Freudian circle — in the previous year he had organized the first Psychoanalytical Congress in Salzburg — were taking a toll of his optimism. The nature of the marital problems is not quite clear, but they were probably due to Jung's susceptibility to the opposite sex. Women found him highly attractive, and a number of female patients fell in love with him. This would probably not have bothered Emma if she could have been sure that Jung remained uninterested in them. But on a trip to Italy in 1907 he had become violently infatuated with an attractive Jewess — an experience he seems to have confided to Freud. Another patient, a twenty-year-old Russian girl named Sabina Spielrein, wanted Jung to become the father of her child, and he seems to have been tempted by the idea. Fortunately, he 'denied himself the pleasure' — as he put it in a letter to Freud — for the girl proved to be violently possessive. Jung was treating her for an obsession with excreta, which led to excessive masturbation and an inability to have a normal sexual relationship; so it is possible that Jung's inclination to make love to her may have been a disinterested desire to effect a cure. At all events, he had reason to be glad he had resisted the temptation, for she went around Zurich claiming he was her lover; he was able to assure Sabina's mother that he had never had sexual intercourse with her, and to ask her for help in putting an end to the gossip. Jung was frank enough to admit to Freud that it was not entirely his patient's fault, and that he was partly to blame.

In March 1909, Jung and Emma visited Freud in Vienna, and there occurred the famous incident of the 'poltergeist in the bookcase'. Where 'occult' phenomena were concerned, Freud was a total sceptic. By 1909, it had become apparent to serious students of psychical research that poltergeists — spirits that throw things — are usually associated with disturbed adolescents, and this had given rise to the theory that the poltergeist activities were somehow caused by the unconscious mind of the adolescent — a kind of 'exteriorization', so to speak, of fierce inner conflicts. Jung believed in this theory, and called poltergeist activity 'exteriorization phenomena'. As Freud and Jung were arguing about the reality of the paranormal, there was suddenly a loud explosion from the bookcase, which made both of them jump. 'There!', said Jung, 'That is an example of the exteriorization phenomenon.' 'Bosh!' said Freud. 'It is not', said Jung, 'And to prove my point, I now predict that in a moment there will be another.' As he said this, there was a second explosion in the bookcase. From a letter he subsequently wrote to Jung, it seems that Freud was more than half convinced. But afterwards, he heard such sounds several times, and concluded that there was some natural cause. Jung was convinced that *he* caused it because he felt his diaphragm growing hot as he and Freud argued. Freudian commentators have always insisted that the noises were merely due to the wood of the bookcase drying out. At this date is is impossible to know what really happened.

Jung's professional life in Zurich was not going as smoothly as he might have wished. Although Bleuler now accepted most of Freud's theories, he seems to have had quiet reservations about Jung, and twice passed him over when it came to an appointment to a teaching post. But there was compensation for the disappointment when Jung was invited to lecture at Clark University in America. Jung's phrasing in his autobiography has a touch of disingenuousness: 'I had been invited to lecture on the association experiment at Clark University in Worcester, Massachusetts. Independently, Freud had also received an invitation . . . ' In fact, Freud was asked first, and Jung was almost certainly asked because he was known as a Freudian, not for his independent researches.

In Bremen there occurred the event already referred to

— Freud's fainting fit as Jung discussed the peat bog corpses. Freud's suggestion that Jung had a 'death wish' towards him was always indignantly denied by Jung, who pointed out that he had exposed himself to ridicule and anger from his colleagues by openly supporting Freud. Yet is is impossible to read Jung's account of their relationship without feeling that Freud was not entirely mistaken. He had come to represent for Jung a shallow positivism and materialism that was profoundly anti-pathetic to Jung's temperament, so it would have been surprising if Jung had not harboured a deep-down conviction that the world would be a better place without Freud.

This journey to America was to be a watershed in their relationship, and corresponded with Jung's discovery of his true independence — that is, of the foundations of his own depth psychology.

It began with a dream. Jung found himself in a strange house, whose upper storey was furnished in rococo style. He went down to the ground floor, and discovered that it was much older, with medieval furnishings and red brick floors. He found a heavy door that led into the cellar. There he found himself in a vaulted room that dated from Roman times. In a stone slab in the floor, he discovered a ring; when he pulled on it, the slab rose, revealing narrow stairs. Descending these, Jung found himself in a low cave cut in the rock. The floor was covered with dust, bones, and broken pottery; there were two ancient human skulls. At this point, he woke up.

Freud and Jung were passing the time on the boat analyzing one another's dreams. Freud was intrigued by the two skulls which, he insisted, indicated that Jung wanted two people dead. Jung felt this was nonsense, but finally, to satisfy Freud, he said that he thought the skulls were those of his wife and sister-in-law.

The fact that Jung decided he had to lie to Freud indicated a profound change in his attitude. It meant that he had decided that Freud was a fool whose stupidity had to be humoured. This change, according to Jung, came about shortly before the dream episode, when Freud was relating one of his own dreams to Jung. Jung asked for further personal details to enable him to interpret it. Freud gave him an odd look and replied: 'But I cannot risk my authority.' 'At that moment', says Jung, 'he lost it altogether.'

For Jung, the interpretation of his own dream had nothing to do with a death wish. He saw it as a 'structural diagram of the human psyche'. 'It postulated something of an *impersonal* nature underlying the psyche.'

Now if we reconsider the dream, we can see that this interpretation was hardly justified. The simple and obvious interpretation is that it represented Jung's own central aim aim in life — to penetrate deeper and deeper into the mind. Some highly ambitious people have dreams of climbing — mountains or skyscrapers. Jung was a typical romantic; he wanted to descend into some deep underworld of the spirit, away from the trivialities and confusions of the surface. (Alice's dream of falling down a rabbit hole seems to symbolize the same thing.) But why should a basement full of pottery and bones symbolize 'an altogether impersonal nature underlying that psyche'? Why is a basement more impersonal than a Roman cellar or a rococo drawing-room? It is not. But it was important to Jung to believe that it was, for his deepest need was to escape this Freudian trap into which he had fallen. He had become a disciple of Freud because Freud's psychology struck him as deeper than that of Bleuler or Janet. Now he, in turn, needed to go deeper than Freud.

Dreams were always of immense importance to Jung. It had been the memory of a childhood dream that had played a central part in his conversion to Freudianism. At the age of four, Jung had dreamed of being in a meadow and discovering a stone-lined hole in the ground. He had descended a stone stairway, pushed aside a curtain, and found himself in a room with flagstones and a golden throne in the centre. On this throne was a huge object which he first thought to be a tree trunk, fifteen feet high. But it was covered with skin, and at the top was a rounded head, with a single eye gazing upward. He woke in a panic. It was years later, he claims, that he realized it was a huge penis.

And now again, another dream of descending into the depths seemed to contain a different message: that the ultimate 'basement' of the human mind had some connection with man's remote past. This, says Jung, was his first inkling of the 'collective *a priori* beneath the personal   .

psyche' — what he later called the collective unconscious. But this concept would not begin to develop until the following year.

And this was basically Jung's problem in 1909. He was becoming increasingly irritable about Freud. He wanted to make it clear that he was his own man, not merely another Freud hanger-on — like Sandor Ferenczi, who began his lecture in Worcester with a tribute to the Master. In his own lectures on word association tests Jung made no reference to Freud. Yet he had nothing to say that differed profoundly from Freud. It was an irritating and unsatisfying situation, and it can hardly have improved things to see Freud 'in a seventh heaven', revelling in the acclaim. Jung admitted to his wife that his own 'libido' was 'gulping it down in vast enjoyment'. He and Freud, were, he said, the 'men of the hour'. But it was not true; Freud was the man of the hour. Jung was just — in the eyes of his hosts — merely Freud's chief acolyte.

Jung's friend Ernest Jones — whom he had been responsible for introducing to Freud — was disconcerted when Jung told him that he preferred not to probe too deeply into the sex lives of his patients because he might meet them later at the dinner table. For Jones, this was an admission that Jung was more interested in social life than in pursuing the truth. For Jung, it was an expression of his increasing disgust with Freud's single-minded preoccupation with sex.

Back in Zurich after a two month absence, Jung found that he had time on his hands. The number of his patients had diminished — possibly because of the Sabina Spielrein affair. Jung was not greatly concerned — he had no need to be when his wife was a member of a wealthy family. In fact, he resigned his post at the Burghölzli, and moved into a house he had built in Küsnacht, by Lake Zurich. He seems to have been glad of a chance to relax. The dream of the house had apparently revived his interest in archaeology and history. In November, he apologized to Freud for a three week silence, explaining that he had been reading Herodotus and a book on the worship of Priapus, the god of procreation. He had also discovered a four-volume work that afforded him endless delight: Friedrich Creuzer's *Symbols and Mythology of Ancient Peoples*. In his reply, Freud said: 'I was delighted to learn that you are going into mythology . . . I can't wait to hear of your discoveries.' Freud, naturally, assumed that Jung was studying ancient myths in order to unveil their sexual content. 'I hope you will soon come to agree with me that in all likelihood mythology centres on the same nuclear complex as the neuroses.' What Freud failed to grasp was that all this reading of mythology was not merely psychological research; it was an escape into a realm that Jung found far more emotionally satisfying than the study of sexual neurosis. Jung's mind needed to be allowed to range freely over literature and over history; he felt cramped as a mere physician. Eight years of clinical work at the Burghölzli had given him his fill of 'reality'; now he hungered for poetry, for myth, for the 'horns of elfland'.

In this next letter, Jung again had to apologize for keeping Freud waiting so long. After brief preliminaries, he goes on: 'Now to better things — mythology. For me there is no longer any doubt what the oldest and most natural myths are trying to say. They speak quite naturally of the nuclear »sexual] complex of neurosis.' He goes on to tell Freud about the legend of the god Ares committing incest with his mother. Freud replied 'Your letters delight me because they suggest a frenzy of satisfying work.' If Freud had guessed what was emerging from this frenzy of reading he would have been less delighted. In fact, he might have taken warning from a paragraph in Jung's previous letter in which Jung speaks of a legendary race of miners called the Dactyls, and adds that they are 'not primarily phallic, but elemental. Only the great, that is to say the *epic*, gods seem to be phallic.'

Meanwhile, Emma Jung was pregnant again, and two more women had fallen in love with him — Mary Moltzer and Martha Böddinghaus. Mary Moltzer went around blackening the name of her rival. Jung told Freud about this in a letter of September 1910, and there is a distinct note of complacency as he speaks about their 'loving jealousy over me'.

It was in 1910 that Jung stumbled upon two discoveries that abruptly crystallized his idea of the collective unconscious. In a Greek magical papyrus called the *Mithras Liturgy*, he came upon a reference to a tube that hangs down from the sun, and which is the origin of the wind. It reminded him that in 1906, a schizophrenic patient had told him that he saw an erect phallus on the sun, and that 'this was where the wind came from'. He also recalled a painting by an early German artist showing a tube coming down from heaven and passing under the clothes of the Virgin Mary, and the Holy Ghost flying down the tube to impregnate her. Was it possible, he wondered, that these three images all sprang from the same deep source in the unconscious?

In the same year, Jung read about the discovery of a cache of 'soul stones' near Arlesheim, a place he had visited in his childhood. Jung saw them in his mind's eye as oblong and blackish, with the upper and lower halves painted different shades. He suddenly recalled the small wooden figure from the ruler he had placed in a pencil case as a child, and hidden under a beam in the attic. Now it struck him that it had resembled the Greek spirit of convalescence, Telesphoros. It was the thought that he had been unconsciously performing some ancient religious rite that suddenly convinced him that 'there are archaic psychic components which have entered the individual psyche without any direct line of tradition'. In other words, that our unconscious minds contain certain symbols and images that have been, so to speak, transmitted in the genes. Jung was not suggesting, of course, that there is some *general* unconscious that connects all human beings, like a vast underground lake; yet his notion that certain mental images are common to all of us comes very close to it.

Once Jung had formulated this notion of the collective unconscious he had, in effect, broken from Freud. In Freudian psychology, phallic symbols (and vaginal symbols) keep appearing in dreams, art and mythology because sex is the most basic interest in all human beings. This is natural, because the instinct of procreation is a part of the instinct to survive. Freud's theory had a solid biological foundation. What Jung was saying was that religious symbols are also a part of man's 'instinctive' heritage, and that they have a purely mental (or psychic) origin. And such a notion was, in fact, profoundly opposed to the whole spirit of Freud. For Freud, religion was 'biological' in origin. God the Father was a monstrous shadow-image of our real fathers; religion was a sublimation of sexual impulses. Freud came very close to Marx's view that religion is the opium of the people. So Jung's suggestion that religious symbols have some kind of independent psychic reality — that they are, so to speak, already swimming around in the depths of the unconscious mind — was a flat contradiction of Freud's most basic idea. In a letter to Jung of January 1911, Freud says: 'I don't know why you are so afraid of my criticism in matters of mythology. I shall be very happy when you plant the flag of libido and repression in that field and return as a victorious conqueror to our medical motherland.' In retrospect, Freud's innocence is remarkable. For Jung was returning to the 'medical motherland' in the position of a general who has been converted to the religion of the people he has conquered.

By 1911, Jung was breaking out in other ways. Since 1910, he had been treating a serious-faced, attractive young woman named Antonia Wolff, who had been shattered by the death of her father. Like so many of Jung's female patients, she fell in love with him. We have no way of knowing whether Jung ever took any sexual advantage of women who 'transferred' their adoration to him in his early years as a psychoanalyst. But with Toni Wolff, he seems to have decided to take the plunge and acquire himself a mistress. The result was domestic chaos. Emma seems to have found out at a fairly early stage, possibly informed by another of the women who loved her husband. Jung, never one to do things covertly, invited Toni to his house as a regular guest, and apparently expected Emma to make the best of the situation. The result was a great deal of bitterness; Emma Jung began a secret correspondence with Freud in which she revealed some of her anguish. Jung, like his contemporary H.G. Wells, obviously felt that a man of genius ought to be permitted infidelities in the name of self-development. Emma, like Wells's wife Catherine, seems to have allowed herself to be reluctantly convinced; but all her instincts revolted. The result, as Jung told Freud in a letter, was that things became 'very turbulent at home'. Emma wrote miserably to Freud: 'The women are naturally all in love with him . . . Carl . . . says I should no longer concentrate as before only on him and the children, but what on earth am I to do?'

In spite of these upheavals — which were entirely his own fault — Jung pressed on with the book which he hoped would establish his reputation as an indpendent thinker: *Metamorphoses and Symbols of the Libido*. This began as a commentary on an article that Jung found in the *Archives of Psychology*, in which a young American girl — who used the pseudonym Miss Frank Miller — described 'Some Instances of Subconscious Creative Imagination'. On board a ship from Naples to Pisa, she dreamed three stanzas of a kind of hymn about God's creation of sound, light and love (in that order). She dreamed another poem — an address of a moth to the sun — soon after. Finally, she dreamed the outline of a drama about an Aztec hero who is stung to death by a green snake. Freud would have found nothing but sexual symbols in these dream writings; but Jung was looking for something else.

Symbols of Transformation (as the later English edition is called) is certainly among Jung's most important works; in fact, since it represents his break from Freud, and the first formulation of his own psychology of symbols and archetypes, it could be regarded as the key work of his career. For this reason it deserves careful consideration.

The original title, *Metamorphoses and Symbols of the Libido*, offers a better summary of its aims. Although he is careful to pay lip service to Freud throughout the first half, there is already one major departure from Freudianism: Jung rejects the notion that the libido is a purely sexual energy, pointing out that the craving for food and the need to escape danger are just as basic as the sexual urge; he redefines libido simply as vital energy. But if other urges are equally 'instinctive', then surely we should find symbols of these urges in our dreams and fantasies?

Now one of the most puzzling things about man is that as far back in history as we can trace, he seems to have been a *religious* animal. Why should this be so? Presumably because religion is an attempt to come to terms with the riddle of the universe: with birth and death, hunger and pain, natural catastrophes, the mysteries of nature. Sex is, of course, an integral part of religion, from the fertility ceremonies of aborigines to the Virgin birth. Jung describes a primitive ceremony in which a hole is dug in the ground and surrounded by small bushes — to look like a vagina — then the men dance around it, thrusting their spears into it, shouting 'Not a pit but a cunt'. So perhaps when we encounter sex in ancient myths and primitive rituals, it is not because sex is the most important impulse in our lives, but because it is a part of an even deeper impulse, religion.

When libido — vital energy — is blocked, says Jung, it tries to transform itself into other shapes. Sex is the most obvious. Primitive people are often lazy and depressed; a ceremony like the one described above redirects their energy and gives them again a sense of purpose. It restores their 'reality function' (Jung quotes Janet here).

In spite of the obeisances towards Freud, Jung is obviously contradicting one of Freud's most basic assumptions. What he is saying is that man's *needs* are far wider and deeper than sex. Happiness is a release of the libido, and the libido has many possible channels, the blockage of any one of which may produce neurosis or send the libido into other channels.

Jung's prize exhibit is Miss Miller. She describes how she had written a sea shanty after watching an Italian officer singing on his night watch. She only mentions this officer casually in passing, but Jung sees this as the heart of the matter. 'Miss Miller may have considerably under-estimated the scope of the erotic impressions she had received.' She suppresses her aroused sexual instinct even before it can enter the realm of conscious awareness; in her dream it is sublimated as a poem about God the Father. The sexual form of the libido has simply found another of its natural outlets: religion.

In this particular instance, Jung still seems to be in the grip of his admiration for Freud. 'Miss Miller's problem was the common human problem: How am I to be creative? Nature knows only one answer to that: Through a child . . . But how does one get a child? Here arises the problem which, as experience has shown, is connected with the father, so that it cannot be tackled properly because too much preoccupation with the father at once brings up the incest-barrier . . . ' This is Jung's explanation of why Miss Miller had to suppress her sexual impulse, and it is hardly convincing; after all, if all girls encountered the incest barrier as soon as they thought about children, the earth would remain unpopulated.

But it is when he comes to the lengthy drama about the

Aztec hero that Jung can finally turn his back on Freud and move into the mythical realm that he made his own. In five long chapters, occupying nearly three hundred pages, he analyses Miss Miller's three page 'drama' at enormous length, with excursions into the origin of the hero, symbols of the mother and deliverence from the mother, rebirth and sacrifice. What he is attempting to do, of course, is to convince us that Miss Miller's fantasies are full of unconscious religious and mythical symbols, to which parallels can be found all over the world. The problem here is that he ends by offering so many parallels that the reader becomes increasingly sceptical. Mark Twain has an anecdote about an inventor who explains his invention to a millionaire. After five minutes, the millionaire is anxious to invest. But the inventor wants to convince him that it has dozens of other possibilities, and goes on for an hour. At the end of that time, the millionaire, exhausted and bored, shows him the door. *Symbols of Transformation* tends to produce the same effect. Several pages, for example, are devoted to an analysis of the hero's name, Chi-wan-to-pel. Jung notes its similarity to Popacatapetl, points out that in German 'popo' means posterior, and that 'poop' means to fart. So the hero's name really means 'I produce him from myself', as excrement is produced from the bowels . . .

The problem here is that anyone who feels that Freud's sexual interpretations are often far-fetched is bound to feel that Jung's interpretations are twice as improbable. They usually seem as arbitrary as the reading of tea leaves. In quoting a line from *Paradise Lost* about God creating sound, Miss Miller also quotes the opening: 'Of man's first disobedience . . . ' Why, Jung asks, does she mention man's disobedience? Because what she really has on her mind is sex and sin — in fact, incest . . . Anticipating the objection that there is no deep significance in quoting the first line of a poem as well as a later one, Jung replies: 'the law of psychic causality is never taken seriously enough: there are no accidents . . . It *is* so, and there is very good reason why it is so.' But when it becomes clear that he intends this admonition to apply to every argument in the book, the reader tends to become increasingly restive. Jung describes one of his patients who masturbated in front of him, while making a boring movement with the other forefinger against her left temple. This, says Jung, is the movement primitive man made when he made fire — twirling a stick against another piece of wood. The girl is demonstrating the transformation of one form of libido into another: sexual energy into fire-making. But since the girl was already masturbating with the other hand, it is hard to see why she needed to transform one into another. Freud would probably have said that the significant point was that she was boring the finger against her temple, and that woman regards her vagina as a temple: so, in fact, she was masturbating with both hands . . . Unfortunately, there is little to chose between this interpretation and Jung's.

As an attempt to formulate a convincing alternative to Freud, *Symbols of Transformation* cannot be regarded as a success. With its long footnotes, its quotations in Greek and Latin, its discussions of Babylonian and Egyptian and Hindu mythology, it produces the impression that Jung is trying to bludgeon the reader into submission by sheer intellectual exhibitionism.

Yet if Jung fails to convince as a scientist, he is altogether more successful as an artist. *Symbols of Transformation* is more than a psychological study; it is also a deeply personal statement of conviction. The first thing the reader notices is the bewildering profusion of quotations from various poems, dramas, historical memoirs and works of fiction. It is virtually an anthology of his favourite literature. The method is the same as that used a few years later by T.S. Eliot in *The Waste Land:* to try to place the present in perspective by evoking the background of the past, of other times and other places, of wider horizons and deeper issues. The point emerges particularly clearly when Jung quotes a long passage from St Augustine on the corruption and wickedness of Carthage; Eliot was to quote the same passage in *The Waste Land.* Eliot was concerned with the narrow materialism, the short-sightedness and mediocrity of the twentieth century. For Jung, this narrowness was symbolized by the sexual theory of Freud. So in spite of the lip service paid to Freud, it is obvious from the beginning that Jung finds the sexual theory of neurosis not only narrow and short-sighted but stifling and suffocating. *Symbols of Transformation* is a determined attempt to throw open some windows — or, if necessary, to break them. It is in the same spirit as Blake's protest about Newton, or Yeats's about T.H. Huxley. What emerges very clearly from all the quotations from Goethe and Nietzsche and Hölderlin and Mörike is that Jung's sympathy is with the great poets and visionaries, not with Freud and his mediocre disciples.

In the early chapters of the book, Jung confines his criticisms of Freud to murmurs of disagreement about the libido. In a later chapter called 'The Sacrifice' (which, significantly, quotes more poems than any other) he finally comes out into the open. Quoting Freud's dictum: 'To begin with we know only sexual objects', Jung comments: 'This statement is not much more than a sexual allegory, as when one speaks of male and female electrical connections, screws, etc. All it does is to read the partial truths of the adult into infantile conditions which are totally different. Freud's view is incorrect if we take it literally . . . ' According to Jung, the incest taboo is connected to the notion of the hero's return into his mother's body (for without such a return he cannot be reborn). Ernest Jones records that when Freud read the book, he wrote to Jones about the precise passage 'where Jung went wrong'. This is almost certainly the passage quoted above.

In his autobiography, Jung records that, as he wrote the chapter 'The Sacrifice', he knew it would cost him his friendship with Freud; the result was that he could not touch his pen for two months. 'At last I resolved to go ahead with the writing — and it did indeed cost me Freud's friendship.'

This is not entirely true. Freud read the book in September 1912, and a certain coolness had already developed, partly as a result of a previous misunderstanding, when Freud had hoped Jung would join him for a weekend at Kreuzlingen; in fact, Jung was away and received the letter too late. In September, Jung returned to America, and the Freud circle heard reports that his lectures were critical of Freud. On his return, Jung wrote to Freud to say that he had been making psychoanalysis more acceptable to many people who had been put off by the problem of sexuality. He added that Freud's 'Kreuzlingen gesture' had dealt him a lasting wound. Freud's reply began 'Dear Dr Jung' (instead of the usual 'Dear

Friend'), and remarks irritably: 'You have reduced a good deal of resistance with your modifications, but I shouldn't advise you to enter this in the credit column because, as you know, the further you remove yourself from what is new in psychoanalysis, the more certain you will be of applause and the less resistance you will meet.' That comment about 'what is new' must have made Jung wince.

Freud and Jung met at the Psychoanalytic Congress in Munich in November, and a kind of reconciliation was effected when Freud explained that he had not deliberately sent the invitation to Kreuzlingen two days late. In a letter to Freud soon after this, Jung made a Freudian slip: 'Even Adler's cronies do not regard me as one of yours' when he meant to write 'one of theirs'. (Adler, whose theory of neurosis was based on the 'will to power', had broken with Freud in the previous year.) Freud pointed this out, and Jung's anger finally exploded in a reply which, he must have known, would be like a slap in the face. Freud's technique of treating his pupils like patients, he said, was a blunder. 'In that way you produce either slavish sons or impudent puppies . . . I am objective enough to see through your little trick. You go around sniffing out all the symptomatic actions in your vicinity, thus reducing everyone to the level of your sons and daughters, who blushingly admit the existence of their faults. Meanwhile you remain on top as a father, sitting pretty. For sheer obsequiousness nobody dares to pluck the prophet by the beard and inquire for once what you would say to a patient with a tendency to analyse the analyst instead of himself . . . You see, my dear Professor, so long as you hand out this stuff I don't give a damn for my symptomatic actions; they shrink to nothing compared with the formidable beam in my brother Freud's eye . . . '

This is perhaps the most revealing letter Jung ever wrote. He had put his finger squarely on a basic truth about Freud: that he was obsessed by a need for power, for personal authority. The reason it was so important that the sexual theory — with its crude reduction of religion to father fixations and genius to Oedipus complexes — should become an 'unshakeable dogma' was that it was the foundation of Freud's authority. He was the messiah of his own ersatz religion, and any questioning of that religion might undermine the messiah. But Jung himself was a skilled player in the power game. There is a sense in which *Symbols of Transformation* could be studied as a remarkable piece of what Stephen Potter called One Up-manship. Jung had struggled from poor and unprom- ising beginnings to achieve international eminence; this was due largely to his position as Freud's chief lieutenant. But he had no intention of remaining a mere lieutenant, for the very good reason that he felt his own vision to be wider and deeper than Freud's. What he wanted, ideally, was to remain within the psychoanalytic movement, while being accepted as its leading theoretical thinker — a kind of Plato to Freud's Socrates.

Closer acquaintance with Freud — on the American trip — convinced him that this was impossible. Freud attached far too much importance to personal authority, and his terms were quite clear: accept that sex is the origin of all neurosis or get out. But Jung saw no reason to accept this choice. He felt there was a third possibility: to gently and imperceptibly widen the sexual theory by such slow degrees that he would carry Freud along with him.

When he began *Symbols of Transformation* the prospects looked excellent. Freud had actively encouraged him to study mythology — assuming he meant to annex it for the sexual theory. And there were signs that Freud not only accepted Jung's mythological ideas, but was preparing to claim them as his own. In a letter to Jung of 1 September 1911, Freud says: 'I . . . am planning a short supplement to the Schreber analysis, which I am sure will appeal to *you*. Besides, for anyone with sharp ears, it announces things to come.' This supplement — delivered at the Congress in Weimar later that month — shows that Freud had been influenced by Jung: it states that the unconscious contains 'relics from primitive man'. And the remark that 'for anyone with sharp ears, it announces things to come' was virtually a promise that Freud himself meant to develop this idea. So does another significant phrase in the letter: 'So you too are aware that the Oedipus complex is at the root of religious feeling! Bravo!' That 'you too' may be regarded as a first gentle hint that Freud intended to claim priority. But if that suggestion irritated Jung, it must also have convinced him his plans for 'widening' the sexual theory were succeeding nicely.

But when it came to the point, Jung was not as Machiavellian as he thought. Throughout the first half of *Symbols of Transformation* he achieves a delicate balancing act — sounding Freudian while gently questioning Freud's ideas. But by the time he reached the 'Sacrifice' chapter, he was unable to hold himself in any longer: he had to come into the open with a fundamental disagreement. The result was not a break with Freud; but it suddenly alerted Freud to the danger. At the Munich Congress, a semi-reconciliation was effected when the 'Kreuzlingen misunderstanding' was cleared up. According to Jung, Freud 'let off steam' and 'did not spare him a good fatherly lecture'. But at lunch, Freud suddenly asked Jung — and his colleague Riklin — why they had not mentioned his name in recent publications about psychoanalysis. Jung answered disingenuously that Freud was so famous as the founder of psychoanalysis that it was unnecessary. There followed the discussion about Ikhnaton and patricide — already mentioned — that led to Freud's second fainting fit. As Jung carried Freud into the other room, he says that Freud gave him a look of deep reproach, and murmured 'How sweet it must be to die'.

So now it was war: undeclared, but war nevertheless. In a letter to Jung, Freud said that the attack was due to migraine, but admitted that it was 'not without a psychic factor'. He added: 'A bit of a neurosis that I ought really to look into.' For Jung, such an admission was like the smell of blood. His next letter begins: 'My very best thanks for one passage in your letter, where you speak about "a bit of a neurosis" you haven't got rid of. This "bit" should, in my opinion, be taken very seriously indeed . . . I have suffered from this bit in my dealings with you, though you haven't seen it . . . ' Jung was playing Freud at his own game. Freud's chief weapon was precisely this tendency to psychoanalyse other people and ascribe their actions to hidden neurosis. A paragraph later, Jung makes no bones about his resentment at this trick. 'I am afflicted with the purely human desire to be understood *intellectually* and not be measured by the yardstick of neurosis.' The swords were out. 'As for this bit of neurosis, may I draw your attention to the fact that you open *The Interpretation of Dreams* with the mournful admission of your own neurosis — the dream of Irma's injection — identification with the neurotic in need of treatment. Very significant.' He goes on to remind Freud of how he had once declined to give further information about a dream, protesting that he would lose his authority. 'One thing I beg of you', he goes on, 'take these statements as an *effort to be honest* and do not apply the depreciatory Viennese criterion of egoistic striving for power or heaven knows whatever other insinuations from the world of the father complex. This is just what I have been hearing on all sides these days, with the result that I am forced to the painful conclusion that the majority of psychoanalysts misuse psychoanalysis for the purpose of devaluing others . . . ' But it was not psychoanalysts he was getting at: it was Freud. 'A particularly preposterous bit of nonsense now going the rounds is that my libido theory is the product of anal eroticism. When I consider *who* cooked up this "theory" I fear for the future of analysis.'

Freud began his lengthy reply by assuring Jung that he was not offended by his bluntness; but he devotes most of the letter to discussing the psychoanalytical magazine and yearbook, and ends: 'I am sorry not to be able to discuss your remark on the neuroses of psychoanalysts at greater length, but this should not be interpreted as a dismissal. In one point, however, I venture to disagree most emphatically: you have not, as you suppose, been injured by my neurosis.' So far, Freud was winning hands down; it was Jung who was losing his temper, while Freud remained cool and patronizing. It was soon after this that Jung sent the devastating letter — already quoted — about pulling the prophet's beard.

The result was not the break Jung had expected. Neither of them were yet ready for that. Both had inflicted wounds; both were hoping to inflict more. Adler would have smiled ironically if he could have seen their correspondence; it was the perfect illustration of his own theory of the will to power. But there was to be no more open sparring. Both were like boxers who are too cautious to lower their guard. The correspondence about purely practical matters is formally polite. In June 1913, Freud wrote: 'Jung is crazy but I have no desire for a separation and should like to let him wreck himself first.' This seems a curious sentiment for someone who has 'no desire for a separation'. What it really meant was that Freud had no desire for a separation until he had had a chance to deal Jung a mortal blow.

In the Congress at Munich that year — 1913 — Jung was chairman. But most members present were partisans of either Freud or Jung. Jung used his position to cut short papers by Freud's supporters, and generally caused much indignation by his arbitrary manner. Nevertheless, he was re-elected president of the Association. Freud's reaction was to suggest that the Association should be dissolved, and re-formed without the Swiss group headed by Jung. Jung made things easier by resigning his editorship of the yearbook. In April 1914, he also resigned his presidency of the Association. But these were merely ritual acts. With the 'Beard of the prophet' letter of sixteen months earlier, Jung had already resigned his most precious possession: his friendship with Freud.

Four

Lord of the Underworld

Jung was a man with an extremely healthy ego; but these
conflicts had shaken him to his foundations. It was not
simply that Freud was a father figure, a man for whom he
felt respect and affection. It was that Freud was the most
famous psychologist in Europe, and therefore considerably 'outranked' Jung. George Meredith once remarked:
'In a dissension between man and wife, the one who has
most friends is in the right.' The same is true of
psychologists. Freud had far more friends and supporters
than Jung. Therefore his criticisms smarted, and Jung *felt*
in the wrong even though he was sure he was in the right.
He felt that the psychoanalysts used unfair weapons —
like the suggestion that his libido theory was due to anal
eroticism. Yet he had to admit that Freud's Oedipus
theory — about the son wanting to kill the father — fitted
his case. After the break, Freud described Jung as 'brutal
and sanctimonious'. Jung fiercely resented the implication
that he was a hypocritical, self-seeking Judas, a 'rat'. Yet
there was just enough truth in it to strike home. He *was*
undoubtedly a man who liked his own way, no matter
what the cost to others. He was, for example, carrying on
the affair with Toni Wolff in spite of Emma's misery. For
years he had been using his powerful personality to
convince others of his ideas — as when he converted
Bleuler to Freudianism. Now he was accused of being
merely a coarse bully. And honesty forced him to admit
that the accusation had some foundation.

The self-criticism led to a new atitude of humility
towards his patients; instead of interpreting their dreams
for them, he merely asked them their own opinions. But
this only begged the question. Even if he rejected his
previous tendency to impose his own views, he still had to
find some new framework of ideas.

Two dreams seemed to confirm his views about the 'collective unconscious'. A white bird descended on the table, and turned into a pretty eight-year-old girl. Later, she changed back into a dove, which told him that it could only change into a human being while the male dove was busy with 'the twelve dead'. The 'twelve dead' seemed to have some vague mythological significance, although he had no idea of what it was. In another dream, he was in the avenue of tombs in Arles. The dead kept coming to life as he looked at them. Finally, he came to a tomb with a wooden crusader in chain mail, who seemed undoubtedly dead; but as Jung looked, he stirred a finger. Again, there was a strong sense that the dream was trying to *tell* him something. And if a dream could 'tell' him something, then dreams are not merely explosions of unconscious desires or fears. They must in some sense be *wiser* than the conscious self. And this was what Jung badly needed to believe. He urgently needed support against his self-doubt and self-criticism.

He began collecting stones from beside the lake and built a miniature village, complete with castle and church. It was a more practical version of his adolescent daydream of being lord of a castle. He was instinctively strengthening another aspect of his personality — the practical man, the builder — as he came to doubt the 'intellectual'.

He was, he realized, struggling against mental illness, induced by the undermining of his self-esteem. The evidence was that his dreams were bursting through into his waking life. On a train journey in October 1913, he had a vision of a flood covering all Europe from the North Sea to the Alps, with floating rubble and drowned bodies; then the sea turned to blood. This was not a momentary hallucination; it lasted a whole hour. It came back again two weeks later. In the summer of 1914, he dreamed three times of a wave of cold air descending from the Arctic and freezing all Europe. It must have been almost a relief when the war broke out in August, and he could interpret these visions as premonitions of the catastrophe.

But the hallucinations persisted. 'I stood helpless before an alien world . . . I was living in a constant state of tension; often I felt as if gigantic blocks of stone were tumbling down on me. One thunderstorm followed another. My enduring these storms was a question of brute strength. Others have been shattered by them — Nietzsche, and Hölderlin, and many others.' Jung had seen enough of patients suffering from delusions to know that his own sanity was in danger. Just as a man who has been deprived of sleep for days begins to dream while awake, so a man with a continual psychological 'leak' — an escape of energy due to misery or anxiety — finds that the clear line between rationality and the irrational begins to blur. 'But there was a demonic strength in me, and from the beginning there was no doubt in my mind that I must find the meaning of what I was experiencing in my fantasies. When I endured these assaults of the unconscious I had an unswerving conviction that I was obeying a higher will, and that feeling continued to uphold me until I had mastered the task.'

Jung was fortunate that he was a psychiatrist, with his own patients to deal with; this must have been important in enabling him to maintain a certain detachment. Under this kind of stress, people who are unaccustomed to self-analysis are likely to destroy themselves by giving way to panic. The answer lies in refusing to give way to panic; and Jung knew this instinctively. He was, in a sense, in a fortunate position. Few psychiatrists have the experience of living through madness. It was a time when it was essential for Jung to maintain the distinction between his 'Number 1' and 'Number 2', the sufferer and the onlooker.

Soon after the vision of the floods that turned into blood, Jung made an important decision: to stop struggling, and to submit completely to the fantasies. He describes how, in December 1913, he was seated at his desk, thinking about his fears — that is to say, trying to resist a rising tide of pessimism and panic. 'Then I let myself drop. Suddenly it was as though the ground literally gave way beneath my feet, and I plunged into dark depths. I could not fend off a feeling of panic. But then, abruptly, at not too great a depth, I landed on my feet in a soft, sticky mass. I felt great relief, although I was apparently in complete darkness. After a while my eyes grew accustomed to the gloom, which was rather like deep twilight.' He found himself facing the entrance to a cave, guarded by a dwarf with a leathery skin. He splashed through icy water to the far end of the cave, where he saw a glowing red crystal. He raised this and found a hollow underneath, with a running stream. The corpse of a blond haired youth floated by, with a wound in his head. This was followed by a gigantic black scarab — a symbol of rebirth — and by a red newborn sun rising out of the water. When he tried to replace the stone, blood gushed out of the opening.

Six days later, Jung had another 'dream'. He was in mountainous country with a brown-skinned savage, and they were lying in wait, holding rifles. Siegfried appeared over the mountain top, driving in a chariot of bones; they shot him, and he plunged down, dead. Jung felt deep remorse at killing the hero; then a tremendous downpour of rain began, washing away the blood . . .

On awakening, Jung felt that it was of immense importance to understand the dream immediately; an inner voice told him that unless he could understand it, he should shoot himself — there was a loaded revolver in his drawer. Suddenly, the solution came. The dream was about the international situation — the Germans determined to have their own way. But he had enough penetration — and humility — to see that the dream was also about himself. Jung had struck Freud as very much 'the officer type'. For the past decade he had been driven by a ruthless ambition — 'brutal and sanctimonious'. 'The dream showed me that the attitude embodied by Siegfried, the hero, no longer suited me. Therefore it had to be killed.'

Jung now made what might be regarded as his most important discovery: that he could, in fact, 'dream' while awake, create an inner world of imagination with such vividness that it became a reality. He called it 'active imagination'.

In order to seize hold of these fantasies, I frequently imagined a steep descent. I even made several attempts to get to the very bottom. The first time I reached, as it were, a depth of about a thousand feet; the next time I found myself at the edge of a cosmic abyss. It was like a voyage to the moon, or a descent into empty space. First came the image of a crater, and I had a feeling that I was in the land of the dead. The atmosphere was that of the other world. Near the steep slope of a rock I caught sight of two figures, an old man with a white beard and a beautiful young girl. I summoned up my courage and approached them as I thought they were real people, and listened attentively to what they told me. The old man explained that he was Elijah, and that gave me a shock. But the girl staggered me even more, for she called herself Salome! She was blind. What a strange couple: Salome and Elijah. But Elijah assured me that he and Salome had belonged together from all eternity, which completely astounded me . . . They had a black serpent living with them.

Later, the Elijah figure developed into an old man that Jung called Philemon. He appeared for the first time as a man with the horns of a bull, holding a bunch of keys. He had the wings of a kingfisher. Jung began to paint Philemon — he had made a hobby of painting ever since his teens — and while he was engaged on the painting, found a dead kingfisher in his garden — a 'coincidence' to which he would later give the name synchronicity.

Philemon and other figures of my fantasies brought home to me the crucial insight that there are things in the psyche which I do not produce, but which produce themselves and have their own life. Philemon represented a force which was not myself. In my fantasies I held conversations with him, and he said things which I had not consciously thought. For I observed clearly that it was he who spoke, not I. He said I treated thoughts as if I generated them myself, but in his view thoughts were like animals in a forest . . . It was he who taught me psychic objectivity, the reality of the psyche.

It was, as Jung himself recognized, the most crucial breakthrough of his life. It convinced him, as nothing else could, of the reality of the collective unconscious and its mythological content. The events of that difficult period provided Jung with insights that he would continue to develop for the rest of his life — almost half a century.

Yet before we consider this development, it may be as well to look more closely into the 'confrontation with the unconscious', and to try to understand precisely what had taken place.

We have seen that Jung was, by nature, a romantic, one who is possessed by a sense of the boundless mystery of the universe. The medical profession was for him a second best; he would have preferred to be an archaeologist. It was Krafft-Ebing's words about 'diseases of the personality', and about the undeveloped state of psychiatry, that brought the realization that this was a field into which he could pour all his creative energies. They probably evoked an image of a kind of magician — or at least a Professor Frankenstein — exploring the underground passages of the human soul.

In spite of his enthusiasm, psychiatry must have been something of a disappointment, with its 'organicist' theories and plodding word association tests. Then Jung discovered Freud. What attracted him was not the sexual theory of neurosis, about which he was sceptical from the very beginning, but Freud's vision of the unconscious as a vast underworld. Once again, Jung could see himself as an explorer, like some character out of Jules Verne, descending into an unfathomed blackness where the sun had never penetrated.

Freud soon proved as disappointing as Bleuler and Krafft-Ebing. And once again it was a book that determined Jung's future direction: Creuzer's *Symbols and Mythology*, and he plunged into it as enthusiastically as Yeats plunged into Ancient Irish myths. Jung wanted and needed to find some connection between 'depth psychology' and myth. Blake once said: 'I must create my own system or be enslaved by another man's', and the result was his own strange mythology of symbolic archetypes — Los, Urizen, and so on. Any reader of *Symbols of Transformation* senses immediately that Jung's 'system' was created out of the same compulsion. The long-suppressed romantic was reasserting himself.

The result was the power struggle with Freud — as crude as the battle for dominance between two male stags or apes. Jung's ego was not as invulnerable as Freud's; he was the one who sustained the wounds. Besides which, Freud was surrounded by disciples, all anxious to assure him that he was right and Jung was wrong. Jung was alone, with no one to heal his wounded ego but himself.

Yet in another sense, this was his good fortune. Most of the major 'outsider' figures of the nineteenth century went through the same crisis: the sense of being alone against the world. Some — like Hölderlin and Van Gogh — were destroyed by the strain. Others — like Schiller and Nietzsche — achieved a new synthesis. Jung's problem was to learn to stand alone — a problem Freud never had to face. So Jung evolved, while Freud stood still.

Now what distinguishes Jung from every other major psychologist of the period was his recognition that he contained two people — 'Number 1' and 'Number 2', the everyday self and 'Philemon'. We have seen that this discovery had already been made by the American Thomson Jay Hudson; in *The Law of Psychic Phenomena* he referred to the two 'selves' as 'the objective mind' and the 'subjective mind'. The objective mind is the everyday self, which 'copes' with the external world; the subjective mind deals with man's inner world.

In our own time, the science of split-brain physiology has discovered that these two selves correspond roughly to the left and right cerebral hemispheres of the brain. When the commissure — the knot of nerves — joining the two halves of the brain is severed (to cure epilepsy, for example), the patient turns into *two people*. One split-brain patient tried to hit his wife with one hand while the other held it back; another tried to do up his flies with one hand while the other undid them. Moreover, it seems that the person I call 'I' lives in the left hemisphere (which deals with language and logic). The person who lives in the right hemisphere (which deals with patterns and intuitions) is a stranger. A split-brain patient who banged into a table with the left side of his body (which is connected to the right brain) did not notice the collision. If a split-brain patient is shown some object with the left eye (or, more precisely, the left visual field) connected to the right brain, he cannot state in words what he has just seen. But he *can* write it down with his left hand.

It has been suggested that the right brain is, in fact, the unconscious mind. Other brain specialists have disputed this. But what does seem to be certain is that the right brain is the gateway to the world of the unconscious, as well as being the dwelling place of the 'subjective mind'.

It may be objected that most of us are not split-brain patients. Yet in a vital sense, this is untrue. Except in moments of deep psychological awareness — perhaps of crisis, or excitement, or inspiration — we do not have much contact with that 'other self'. Mozart once said that lengthy tunes were always popping into his head; he obviously meant that they came from the realm of the right brain — which is man's 'artistic' half — into the left brain, the personal ego. If Mozart, with his intuitive genius, was a 'split-brain patient', then the rest of us certainly are.

But although Jung was aware of the presence of two 'selves' inside his head, he never worked out clearly their separate functions. For example, the opening chapter of *Symbols of Transformation* is called 'Two Kinds of Thinking'. The first type is 'directed thinking', thinking in language; this is obviously left-brain thinking. But according to Jung, the second type of thinking, 'undirected thinking', is fantasy, free association — the kind we indulge in as we lie awake in the middle of the night. He equates this with dreaming, and argues that the thinking of primitive man is of this type — this he sees as the origin of myths. In fact, right-brain thinking is *intuitive* thinking, not free fantasy; it is the kind of 'thinking' that enables the artist to 'balance' his composition or the musician to shape his symphony. But it is also the kind of thinking that brings the sudden flash of insight to the scientist and the mathematician. So the two types of thinking cannot be sharply separated.

In the light of this insight, Jung's attempt to argue that 'mythological thinking' is the counterpart of 'directed thinking' sounds altogether less convincing. He seems to be trying to create a distinction that does not really exist — at least, not in the sharp, clear form he suggests. And this in turn undermines his central assertion: 'What, with us, is a subterranean fantasy was once open to the light of day. What, with us, crops up only in dreams and fantasies was once either a conscious custom or a general belief' — an assertion which is the very foundation of his belief in the 'archetypes of the collective unconscious'. Jung's mythological unconscious seems to be less an intuitive insight into the nature of the psyche than a calculated counterblast against Freud's 'sexual unconscious'.

Yet Jung's own intuitive vision of the unconscious is another matter. Like Hudson he recognizes that it is essentially an independent realm, a 'second self'. He also recognizes that it is a realm of tremendous vital forces. Hudson was amazed when a fairly ordinary young man, under hypnosis, proceeded to hold imaginary conversations with philosophers and to create the most brilliant intellectual systems. Jung was astonished to find that his Philemon said things that he himself had not consciously thought. He had succeeded in producing an interesting form of self-hypnosis in which the 'objective mind' ('Number 1') was permitted to enter the realm of the subjective mind ('Number 2').

All this enables us to pinpoint the essential difference between Freud and Jung — which also happens to be the difference between Freud and Janet, and Freud and Hudson. For Freud, the unconscious is simply the dark depths of the psyche, full of 'infantile material' which periodically rises to the surface and creates a hazard for shipping. It gives trouble in the same way that the appendix — another 'archaic' organ — sometimes gives trouble. But, like the appendix, it seems to have no positive function.

For Jung, the unconscious was full of mysterious, life-giving forces. (Hudson recognized that the 'subjective mind' is in charge of our vital energies.) All true poetry, all true art, has its origin in the unconscious, and this explains its quality of freshness, of vitality, of 'surprise'. According to Hudson, neurosis is due to loss of contact between the subjective and objective minds. The objective mind, entangled in its own egotistical little purposes, forgets that it has an invisible partner — an immense source of power — and begins to find life dull, arduous and repetitive. The result is a kind of 'negative feedback', loss of desire leading to loss of motivation. Yet the resultant anguish is unnecessary. The subjective mind has not really abandoned us. It is perfectly willing to come to the rescue with an unexpected burst of vitality or sensation of comfort. As the spirit tells Faust:

> 'The spirit world shuts not its gates;
> Your heart is closed, your senses sleep . . . '

And it was Jung's recognition that the unconscious is what Goethe called 'the spirit world' (*die geisterwelt*), and that it is nothing less than our connection with the wellsprings of life, that distinguished his concept so clearly from Freud's. Where the psyche is concerned, Jung is a romantic optimist and Freud is a 'realist' pessimist. Jung's view of the unconscious is almost Chestertonian; he feels that its basic message is one of 'absurd good news'.

When Jung retreated to Küsnacht after the break with Freud, it was not merely to lick his wounds and repair his damaged ego. The task that faced him was of self-renewal, a total change of direction. The Freudians accused him of being a self-seeking, self-promoting egoist, whose mythological theory was a blatant attempt to steal Freud's ideas and dress them up with his own mythological embellishments. Jung was honest enough to recognize that there was more than a grain of truth in this. It was the old moral issue that tormented Nietzsche so much: is the thinker driven by a desire for truth, or merely a desire to be regarded as a great thinker? Jung had to be prepared to abandon the old Jung, the Jung the Freudians were attacking, and become another person. This meant that he had to be *absolutely sure* of the truth of what he was saying.

And this was rather a tall order for someone who had once swallowed most of the Freudian dogmas. If Freud was wrong to see phalluses and vaginas and incest wishes in the simplest dream, how could Jung be sure that his own talk about heroes and rebirth was not just as absurd?

And it was in this extremity of self-doubt that his unconscious — the subjective mind — came to the rescue, filling his dreams with mythological symbols that seemed to support his theory of archetypes — dead knights in armour, Siegfried, Salome, Elijah, Philemon. His Freudian opponents might have pointed out that Jung had spent years immersing himself in mythology and its symbols, and that it would hardly be surprising if they turned up in his dreams. No doubt Jung was haunted by the same debilitating suspicion. But the waking dreams must have seemed an altogether different matter. To be able to enter his own unconscious mind and *hold conversations* with his 'Number 2' was an experience that left no room for doubt. If Freud had more friends than Jung, Jung had a single ally who was worth more than all of them.

Jung wrote down his fantasies in a volume he called the Black Book; later, he transferred them to the Red Book, and added drawings and paintings. These paintings are extremely impressive, revealing that Jung could probably have made a career as an artist.* But one of the most

* Some are reproduced in *Jung: Word and Image*, edited by A. Jaffé, 1979

obvious and striking things about them is that they are full
of religious imagery — not simply from Christianity, but
from the religions of the east. A watercolour of Philemon
looks exactly like part of an illuminated manuscript of the
Middle Ages. A painting of the Hindu creator of the
world, Prajapati, looks as if it has been taken from some
Tibetan manuscript. A painting of 'The Light at the Core
of the Darkness' shows a Chinese-looking dragon emerging from the explosion of light; but below there is a typical
Swiss village. A mandala floating in the air above a
beautifully painted town on the edge of a lake again
combines eternal religious symbolism with the world of
the twentieth century — the town is full of soldiers, and
tall chimneys belch industrial smoke. It is as if Jung is
turning to the world's religions for aid.

But perhaps the most significant of these paintings, in
the light of Jung's psychological problems, is the one
called 'Encounter with the Shadow'. It shows a figure with
a face like an animal, dressed in an elaborate opera cloak
or Chinese robe, standing in the corner of a red-tiled
room, with a mandala symbol behind him. For Jung, the
'shadow' is the unconscious mind: not the *whole* unconscious, but a part of us that is waiting, so to speak, to
emerge into the light of day and take his place as part of
the conscious personality. What seems significant is that
Jung here represents the shadow as a rather sinister
looking figure, a little like Jack the Ripper skulking in a
dark corner. Yet he also recognized the brown-skinned
savage who helped him to kill Siegfried as his shadow. If
we regard him as an image of Hudson's 'subjective mind',
or the right brain, we can see immediately how appropriate it is that he is a brown-skinned savage. The right brain
is our intuitive part; it *is* simple, primitive and child-like;
and it is quite clearly distinguished from the left-brain ego,
with its command of language and logic. In recognizing
the brown-skinned savage as his shadow, we can see that
Jung had intuitively grasped the nature of the 'second
self', the subjective mind. But his mental image of the
shadow, as depicted in his painting, is altogether more
sinister — in a word, more Freudian. Jung's Freudian
preconceptions are still distorting his intuitions.

Yet the Red Book is a proof of the success of Jung's
attempt at self-renewal. He was creating another self that

had more in common with a medieval monk than a modern psychiatrist. Even the building of the model village and the church reveals the same determination to turn his back on the Freudian intellectual and to conjure into existence a simpler, more primitive aspect of his personality. He was 'realizing' the shadow.

In 1916, Jung added a new strand to that new personality by writing a short book called *Seven Sermons to the Dead*. In *Memories, Dreams, Reflections*, he explains that it began with a feeling of restlessness, and the sensation that the air was filled with ghostly entities. 'Then it was as if my house began to be haunted. My eldest daughter saw a white figure pass through her room. My second daughter, independently . . . related that twice in the night her blanket had been snatched away . . . ' Two days later, the front door bell began ringing violently, but there was no one there. Jung was apparently producing 'exteriorization phenomena' — poltergeist effects. He felt he was surrounded by the dead, and began to write the *Seven Sermons*. When it was finished, three evenings later, the 'haunting' was over.

Anyone who turns to the *Seven Sermons* expecting revelations will be disappointed. A cynic might say that it was Jung's attempt to write his own *Thus Spake Zarathustra*. He explains that 'archetypes speak the language of high rhetoric, even of bombast'. But the simpler explanation is that someone who wants to write 'impersonally', in a voice unlike that of his left-brain ego, is likely to imitate that impersonal language of mankind that is found in the world's scriptures.

> The dead came back from Jerusalem, where they found not what they sought. They prayed me let them in and besought my word, and thus I began my teaching.
> Harken: I begin with nothingness. Nothingness is the same as fullness. In infinity, full is no better than empty . . .

In the second sermon, the dead echo Zarathustra when they ask 'Is God dead?' Jung explains that God is 'creatura', the creation, and that the devil is the opposite of God: the void. But there is a third member of the trinity: Abraxas, life itself, with a dual face of good and evil, like the Hindu deity Kali. At the end of the sixth sermon, the dead say: 'Cease this talk of gods and daemons and souls. At bottom this hath long been known to us.' It seems that the previous sermons have been a waste of breath. Yet in the seventh sermon occurs one of the most significant lines of all: 'In this world is man Abraxas, the creator and destroyer of his own world.'

For a scientist, it seems an extraordinary statement. But then, as we have seen, Jung was not really a scientist by temperament; he has very little in common with Newton or Einstein. Jung was a romantic and something of a mystic. In the *Seven Sermons* he dons the mantle of Zarathustra — although the content has more in common with the Hermetic writings than with Nietzsche. The statement that man is the creator and destroyer of his own world is, in effect, an admission that he sees himself partly as artist, partly as prophet. And the whole book suggests a man with a mission rather than a scientist. Yet it is significant that Jung did not allow the *Seven Sermons* to be printed during his lifetime (except in a small private edition for his own use); where the public was concerned, he wished to be regarded purely as a scientist.

All this raises again the question we have discussed in the Introduction. It may seem perfectly reasonable that Jung should have wished to be known solely as a scientist; after all, he had his career to think about. Yet on closer examination there seems to be rather more to it than that. Jung was something of an artist by temperament, and no scientist needs to be ashamed of having a streak of the artist in his composition (indeed, it is interesting to note how many scientists and mathematicians are also good musicians, as if there was a need to create an internal balance between feeling and reason). And during the period of the 'confrontation with the unconscious', he deliberately strengthened the artist in his composition, carving stone, painting pictures, writing the *Sermons*. By 1920, he was experimenting with the *I Ching*. The curious poltergeist effects of 1916 had deepened his certainty of the existence of the paranormal. He had also become increasingly fascinated by the religious symbol of the mandala (which is Sanskrit for circle), seeing it as an image of the soul. The autobiography contains the following curious passage:

It was only towards the end of the First World War that I gradually began to emerge from the darkness. Two events contributed to this. The first was that I broke with the woman who was determined to convince me that my fantasies had artistic value; the second and principal event was that I began to understand mandala drawings. This happened in 1918-19 . . . In 1918-19 I was in Chateau d'Oex as Commandant de la Région Anglaise des Internés de la Guerre. While I was there I sketched every morning in a notebook a small circular drawing, a mandala, which seemed to correspond to my inner situation at the time. With the help of these drawings I could observe my psychic transformations from day to day. One day, for example, I received a letter from that aesthetic lady in which she again stubbornly maintained that the fantasies arising from my unconscious had artistic value and should be considered art. The letter got on my nerves. It was far from stupid and therefore dangerously persuasive. The modern artist, after all, seeks to create art out of the unconscious. The utilitarianism and self-importance concealed behind this thesis touched a doubt in myself, namely, my uncertainty whether the fantasies I was producing were really spontaneous and natural, and not ultimately my own arbitrary inventions. I was by no means free from the bigotry and hubris of consciousness which wants to believe that any half-way decent inspiration is due to one's own merit, whereas inferior reactions come merely by chance, or even derive from alien sources. Out of this irritation and disharmony within myself there proceeded, the following day, a changed mandala: part of the periphery had burst open and the symmetry was destroyed.

And Jung broke with the 'aesthetic lady' — a curiously violent reaction.

Jung's explanation of his irritation looks convincing at a casual glance, but examined more closely it proves to be almost meaningless. He is worried, he says, whether the paintings were really spontaneous and natural, or conscious inventions. Then he adds that there was an element in himself that *wanted* to believe they were conscious inventions, and not 'inferior reactions come merely by chance, or . . . from alien sources'. This hardly makes sense.

It is all the more puzzling because the lady's reaction to his paintings will probably be that of most people; Jung is a good painter, in a crude, primitive way; he often brings to mind the work of Ensor. Why *did* her admiration so irritate him that he broke with her?

A moment's thought uncovers the answer. The artist *invents*. Jung did not want to believe that his paintings were 'inventions' in that sense; he wanted to believe that they were the authentic voice of the unconscious. We may recall that key sentence from *Symbols of Transformation:* 'the law of psychic causality is never taken seriously enough: there are no accidents . . . ' So in suggesting that Jung was an artist, the unnamed woman was — quite innocently — offering him the deadliest of all insults. If his paintings were art, they were 'inventions'. If his paintings were inventions — and here we come to the heart of the matter — then the same could apply to the whole theory of mythological symbols expressed in *Symbols of Transformation*. The lady's 'compliment' was virtually a repetition of the accusation hurled at him by Freud and his followers. And it obviously struck home.

This raises the central question: *was* the whole theory of 'archetypes' (as he came to call them in 1919) a mere projection of Jung's need to turn his back on the sexual theory? It must be frankly acknowledged that, in *Symbols of Transformation*, the case is argued so badly that it is tempting to answer: yes. We may recall that in 1906 Jung was struck by a schizophrenic patient's remark that the sun had an erect penis and that this was the source of the wind; four years later he came upon the Mithraic liturgy mentioning that the source of the wind is a tube hanging down from the sun. On closer examination, this is hardly convincing. In a hot country, primitive people — who worshipped the sun — might well have a myth that the wind (which is hot) comes from the sun; if so, then it must either come from the sun's 'mouth' — and the sun obviously does not possess a mouth — or from some sort of tube. There is no connection here with an erect penis.

Jung's arguments for the mythological theory are also less than convincing. He states that there was a time in the ancient world 'when . . . fantasy was legitimate truth'. He instances a child's daydream that he is really a prince in disguise, and compares this to such ancient myths as Romulus and Remus, Semiramis and Moses in the bullrushes. 'The fantasy therefore chooses . . . a classical form which at one time had real validity.' Similarly, he says, a fantasy of a burglar breaking into a house and committing rape (presumably a woman's fantasy) can be paralleled in mythology in the story of Persephone, Deianira, Europa and so on.

Our reaction to all this is understandable scepticism. Is he trying to tell us that when a child daydreams of being a prince, he is responding to some mythological archetype in his unconscious mind, and that when a woman daydreams of rape she is somehow inspired by ancient myths of seduction? This is clearly preposterous: the child can daydream of being a prince without any help from mythological archetypes. The fantasy is not 'choosing a classical form'; it is choosing a completely natural form. And the same applies with twice as much force in the case of the rape fantasy, since sex is the most powerful of natural impulses.

What we have to grasp is that the feeble argument fails to do justice to Jung's basic conception. What he is saying, in fact, is that man is a *religious* animal as well as a sexual animal, and that religious needs are as powerful and genuine as sexual needs — in fact, more so, since they can often suppress the sex needs. So when we plunge down into the world of the unconscious, we are likely to find religious needs reflected there as much as sexual needs. We shall also find other basic needs — ambition, for example, the driving force of the hero. So it would be more accurate to say that the story of Romulus and Remus or of Moses in the bullrushes reflects the same craving as the child's fantasy about being a prince in disguise, rather than vice versa.

At this stage of his career, Jung was still struggling to express certain intuitive perceptions, and was far from doing so with the success he achieved in later life. This can be clearly seen in his only important work of the period, an essay called 'The Transcendent Function' — unpublished at the time.* Amusingly enough, he fails to explain what he means by 'the transcendent function', although he periodically sounds as if he is about to define it. The unconscious, he says, is frequently in conflict with the conscious mind. And 'the answer lies in getting rid of the separation between conscious and unconscious' (a con-

---

* Later published in Volume 8 of the *Collected Works*, p.67.

cept he later called 'individuation'). The transcendent function seems to be a kind of 'will to health' in the patient, which must be dragged into the light of day. For example, an unmarried woman patient told Jung that she had dreamed that someone gave her a richly ornamented antique sword, dug up from a tumulus. When asked about associations, she told Jung that her father had once flashed his dagger in the sunlight. He was an energetic, strong-willed man who had many love affairs, and he died when she was young. But although she obviously had a strong father complex, with sexual fantasies about him, she was inclined to 'identify' with her mother. So in choosing men, she was inclined to choose weak and neurotic males.

Now if Freud had been analysing this case, he would obviously have seen the sword as a phallic symbol, and assumed that the patient's illness was due to her repression of the incestuous impulse — hence her preference for weak men. Jung went an important step further. So far, the patient had herself been weak and neurotic. Through the image of the sword, her unconscious was trying to tell her that she too could be strong and healthy, like her father. In short, Jung's interpretation offered her a *course of action*. The sword represented her will to health — her 'transcendent function'.

In his later work, Jung is willing to recognize that the 'transcendent function' is man's religious drive, the craving to evolve to a higher level. He can accept the Freudian notion that the unconscious is full of 'infantile material', for he recognizes that one of our problems is the child still inside us — sometimes spoilt, sometimes nervous, miserable, self-pitying, but always essentially *passive*. The 'transcendent function' is the part of the unconscious that urges us to evolve — towards the hero, the saint or the sage. But in 1916, Jung was still struggling towards this synthesis; the result is that the reader often has to guess what he is trying to say.

Yet the main achievement of these years, as Jung himself realized, was the recognition of the importance of the mandala symbol. He writes:

During those years, between 1918 and 1920, I began to understand that the goal of psychic development is the self.

There is no linear evolution; there is only a circumambulation of the self. Uniform development exists, at most, only at the beginning; later, everything points towards the centre. This insight gave me stability, and gradually my inner peace returned. I knew that in finding the mandala as an ultimate expression of the self, I had attained what was for me the ultimate. Perhaps someone else knows more, but not I.

At first, this seems baffling — the self as a circle — until we recollect the basic yin-yang symbol of the *I Ching* — a circle divided into white and black halves. Jung saw this as a symbol of the mind, divided into conscious and unconscious. But what does Jung mean in saying that 'the answer obviously consists in getting rid of the separation between conscious and the unconscious'? The answer can be grasped if we turn back to Thomson Jay Hudson. According to Hudson, genius is an ideal collaboration between the objective and subjective minds; in a Shakespeare, they are so closely in touch that intuitions from the subjective mind are swiftly and easily translated into the language of the objective mind, while the subjective mind also responds swiftly and accurately to the demands of the objective mind. There is no 'separation', as there is in intellectuals, or in neurotics whose objective and subjective minds are inclined to go their separate ways. It is this close cooperation between the two 'selves' that Jung means by 'individuation'.

For Jung, personally, individuation meant the ability to surrender himself to the 'subjective mind' — as in the waking fantasies he called 'active imagination'. We can also see it in his daily use of mandalas — in the internment camp — to gain insight into his own 'psychic transformations'. In effect, he had learned how to allow his 'other self' to take charge of the hand holding the pencil, and to express itself freely in symbols, the natural language of the right brain.

The 'confrontation with the unconscious' had provided Jung with what he needed so badly: a creative alternative to the sexual theory of neurosis.

Five

The Invisible Writing

By 1919, Jung had not merely made a complete recovery; he had achieved a new level of vitality and self-confidence. Brome remarks: 'Those who knew him recall the absolute conviction with which he began to speak of the collective unconscious, the anima, the self and individuation.' During the war he had struck his children as distant and detached; now suddenly he began playing with them and taking them on camping expeditions. He had more patients than ever. And, more than ever, he was surrounded by adoring women. He seemed to have much the same power over women as another remarkable contemporary, Gurdjieff, and for much the same reason. One woman wrote: 'He gave the impression of great power and insight, and I was altogether shattered at the idea that he would see right through me, even into the sexual fantasies that were tormenting me.' And, like Gurdjieff, Jung seems to have had no inhibitions about accepting the homage, and bestowing his favour on selected members of the harem. One mistress told Brome: 'Given a summer's evening, a private place looking out on the lake and he would quote something in that deep resonant voice of his and look at a woman like a young girl he had just fallen in love with on a spring day.' Jung firmly resisted all efforts of Toni Wolff to persuade him to divorce Emma and marry her. She would probably have been unwilling to allow him the freedom that Emma had finally been forced to concede. Besides, Emma was an admirable wife and mother, and Jung loved his home.

It may have been to escape the women that Jung accepted an offer from a businessman friend to accompany him to North Africa. He arrived in Algiers in March 1920, and went on to Tunis alone. This African holiday was to be one of the most important experiences of his life.

Here he was in his element, surrounded by reminders of Roman occupation, of Christian origins, of the past greatness of the Arabs. He was also convinced that the soil smelt of the blood that had soaked into it over the centuries. Even the openly flaunted homosexuality of the Arabs reminded him of 'an infinitely more naive world of adolescents who were preparing, with the aid of slender knowledge of the Koran, to emerge from their original state of twilight consciousness.' Everything in North Africa made Jung feel that he was closer to the twilight consciousness of mankind.

The key to the impact of North Africa lies in Jung's comment: 'While I was still caught up in this dream of a static, age-old existence, I suddenly thought of my pocket watch, the symbol of the European's accelerated tempo.' This timeless world of North Africa, where punctuality was no longer a virtue, brought him closer to that world of myth and the unconscious whose existence he had only sensed in Switzerland, the home of the cuckoo clock. One of the most interesting discoveries of split-brain physiology is that the right brain has no sense of time; it is the left that is obsessed by time. Westerners are natural 'left-brainers'; Arabs seem to be natural 'right-brainers'. In his book *The Dance of Life** the anthropologist Edward T. Hall describes western man's time sense as 'monochromatic', meaning 'in a straight line'; the Arabs, Turks, the Indian tribes of South America, have a 'polychromatic' time sense; for them, time is more like a web, stretching out in all directions. In fact, we can all experience time as a 'web' when we relax deeply and forget all sense of urgency. But it is difficult for a westerner to relax naturally; he lives in a permanent state of tension. Jung, with his Swiss sense of order and his Germanic efficiency, was more of a 'left-brainer' than most. So for him, lengthy contact with a 'polychromatic' race brought a deep sense of peace and harmony.

The problem, of course, is that 'right-brainers' tend to be less efficient; T. E. Lawrence remarked of the Arabs: 'Their less taut wills flagged before mine flagged.' Jung was deeply impressed by a scene he witnessed near an oasis, when a local landowner had hired hordes of desert

* 1983.

nomads to dig irrigation ditches. He watched with
amazement as they dug frantically in the hot sun, as
others established a work rhythm by beating drums; at
dusk they all dropped in exhaustion beside their camels
and slept until dawn. Jung could see that their work had
been ritualized because they lacked the will-drive to apply
an intense individual effort. These people worked like a
single organism. It brought again the recognition that
western man had become split off from the rest of society,
and that this is bound to affect our whole notion of the
psyche. As Eliot says: 'We each think of the key, each in
his prison.' Yet the 'prison' may be an artificial condition,
created by stress. It seemed to be a verification of Jung's
intuition that there is a different kind of consciousness,
joining human beings rather than separating them.

Back home in Küsnacht, Jung began his experiments
with the *I Ching*. This represented the most complete
change of direction that Jung had experienced since he
decided to become a psychologist more than twenty years
earlier. In spite of his interest in the occult, Jung had
remained basically a scientific sceptic where the ancient
'magical' tradition was concerned. Yet 'coincidences' —
like the discovery of the dead kingfisher in his garden
when he was making a painting of Philemon as a
kingfisher — deepened his intuitive certainty that the
psyche is not governed by the laws of chance. His visions
of blood in 1913 seemed to be genuine instances of
precognition of the future — and by any scientific
criterion, precognition is an impossibility. Jung tried the *I
Ching* on a patient, a young man with a mother complex
who was thinking of marrying a rather strong-minded
girl. The *I Ching* answered: 'The maiden is powerful. One
should not marry such a maiden.' He asked a Chinese
philosopher what he thought of the *I Ching*, and the
philosopher (Hu Shih) dismissed it as an old book of
spells. But later he told Jung the story of a friend, involved
in an unhappy love affair, who went to a Taoist temple
one day to consult the oracle. 'And was it correct?' asked
Jung. 'Of course, was the reply.'

To accept such things would seem to classify Jung with
people who read their horoscopes in newspapers or refuse
to travel on Friday the 13th. And clearly, Jung was not
such a person. What was happening was that his universe

was being steadily transformed by a deepening intuition that the psyche interacts in some mysterious and unknown way with the world around us. It could be compared to the feeling of primitive man that he is surrounded by spirits and gods. But in Jung, this notion took the form of the intuition that we also somehow *contain* the spirits and gods, and that there are forces deep inside us that can somehow be brought into harmony with the forces outside us.

The motive force that had fuelled Jung's search could be defined as a form of romanticism; but romanticism in its deepest sense, as defined in a remark made by Arthur Koestler: 'In my youth I regarded the Universe as an open book, printed in the language of physical equations, whereas now it appears to me as a text written in invisible ink, of which, in our rare moments of grace, we are able to decipher a small fragment.' Every major romantic has possessed this intuition: that the secret of the universe is somehow written in invisible writing.

At the same time, it is important to grasp that Jung was no expert at deciphering 'invisible writing'. He was a deeply intuitive man — which is why he was such a good doctor — who was not particularly skilled at turning insights into words. *Symbols of Transformation* was a clumsy attempt to express this feeling that the secret is written in invisible writing, and it has something of the obscurity of a Gnostic text. And in book after book, we feel he is fumbling towards an insight rather than pursuing it with single-minded determination.

This is nowhere more plain than in Jung's next major work, *Psychological Types*, which appeared in 1921. It has become Jung's best-known work, because of its introduction of the terms 'introvert' and 'extravert'; yet to anyone familiar with Jung's earlier work, it must have seemed to signal a complete change of direction. Instead of mythology, symbolism and the unconscious, we have a system of classification that seems to be a throwback to the Elizabethan notion of 'humours'.

In his autobiography, Jung is curiously reticent about the origin of the book, although he says that he was 'busy with preparatory work' as early as 1916. The major clue lies in the book itself — the fourth chapter — in which he discusses the theories of a certain Dr Furneaux Jordan, who in 1896 published a book called *Character as Seen in Body and Parentage*. Jung remarks that his attention was drawn to the book by a London colleague, Dr Constance Long; we know that he went to London to lecture in July 1919. It therefore seems possible that this was when he encountered the book.

It is Jordan who was responsible for inventing the notion of extraverts and introverts; he states that there are 'two generic fundamental biases in character', which could be labelled the active and the reflective. Jung's chapter on Jordan is mostly devoted to criticism, and he nowhere acknowledges his basic indebtedness to Jordan; on the other hand, neither does he state anywhere that he had invented the classifications of extravert and introvert before he read Jordan.

One of the best summaries of *Psychological Types* is offered by Jung himself in his essay 'Approaching the Unconscious' — the last thing he wrote. Here he says:

> Extraversion and introversion are just two among many peculiarities of human behaviour. But they are often rather obvious and easily recognisable. If one studies extraverted individuals, for instance, one soon discovers that they differ in many ways from one another, and that being extraverted is therefore a superficial and too general criterion to be really characteristic. That is why, long ago, I tried to find some further basic peculiarities — peculiarities that might serve the purpose of giving some order to the apparently limitless variations in human individuality.
>
> I had always been impressed by the fact that there are a surprising number of individuals who never use their minds if they can avoid it, and an equal number who do use their minds, but in an amazingly stupid way. I was also surprised to find many intelligent and wideawake people who lived (as far as one could make out) as if they had never learned to use their sense organs: they did not see the things before their eyes, hear the words sounding in their ears, or notice the things they touched or tasted. Some lived without being aware of the state of their own bodies.
>
> There were others who seemed to live in a most curious state of consciousness, as if the state they had arrived at today were final, with no possibility of change, or as if the world and the psyche were static and would remain so forever. They seemed devoid of all imagination, and they entirely and exclusively depended upon their sense percep-

tion. Chances and possibilities did not exist in their world, and in 'today' there was no real 'tomorrow'. The future was just a repetition of the past.

I am trying here to give the reader a glimpse of my own first impressions when I began to observe the many people I met. It soon became clear to me, however, that the people who used their minds were those who *thought* — that is, who applied their intellectual faculty in trying to adapt themselves to people and circumstances. And the equally intelligent people who did not think were those who sought and found their way by *feeling*.

We may speculate, then, that Jung's discovery of Jordan's book produced an intellectual explosion, and that his dissatisfaction with Jordan's further attempt to subdivide the two basic types — active and reflective — led to the recognition that introvert and extravert could also be subdivided into four further categories: thinking, feeling, sensation and intuition. ('Feeling' means here only a non-linguistic approach to problems, such as when we say: 'I feel the easiest solution would be . . .') *Psychological Types* is an attempt to illustrate the eight types ('Introverted-feeling type', 'extraverted-feeling type', etc) with characters from history and fiction. In fact, he soon finds it necessary to create still further subdivisions, until a reader begins to suspect that he is losing his way.

Yet although, in summary, *Psychological Types* sounds like a radical departure from Jung's earlier preoccupations, the book itself makes a totally different impression. It begins with a lengthy comparison between two early Church Fathers, Tertullian and Origen — examples of the introverted and extraverted thinking types. And we soon feel — just as in *Symbols of Transformation* — that they are far more than mere illustrations of a thesis: Jung is discussing them because he feels profoundly at home in the world of the early Christian Church. When Anatole France — whom Jung once admired — talks about the early Church, it is in a spirit of ironic scepticism, poking gentle fun at the ascetics who tormented their bodies instead of appreciating the delights of the senses. When Jung talks about the early Church, he obviously feels that these men were concerned with important issues that the modern world has forgotten; once again, the modern reader is struck with the kinship with T. S. Eliot. And after discussing the problem of transubstantiation, nominalism and realism, and the controversy between Luther and Zwingli, he goes on to talk about Schiller, Goethe, Nietzsche and Carl Spitteler's *Prometheus and Epimetheus*. It is as if he is saying: Freud tried to reduce life to sex and infantile repressions, but *this* is what is really important . . .

In short, Jung is still making his major points indirectly rather than directly; it takes him more than four hundred pages to reach his discussion of the introverted and extraverted types in Chapter 10. Yet the major point emerges very clearly, for all that. What all these people have in common is that for them, as for Jung, the world is full of 'invisible writing'. What is so interesting about *Psychological Types* is that it is written on two levels: that of an old-fashioned, pre-Freudian textbook of psychology, and of a deeply personal 'confession of faith'. It is probably the piquancy of the contrast between the two that has made this Jung's most famous book.

A patient of Jung's, Dr Liliane Frey-Rohn, later made the interesting comment: 'He wrote in a crabbed small hand when he was a dry and scientific writer, expanding into a much more open work style as he gathered confidence in his theories, and later using on occasion a beautiful exact Gothic script like a medieval manuscript.' In that sense, *Psychological Types* is still written in a small, crabbed handwriting. But even before it was published, he was extending his intuitions towards new horizons. After his early experiments with the *I Ching*, he read the new translation and commentary by Richard Wilhelm, a Christian missionary who had gone to China and become a total convert to the ancient Chinese culture. When Wilhelm came to Zurich in 1922, the two men met, and became close friends. They seem to have spent much of their time together experimenting with the *I Ching*: on one occasion, the oracle warned Jung not to take what would happen the next day too seriously; in fact, an old friend was killed in a car crash.

It was also in 1922 that Jung bought a piece of land by the lakeside at Bollingen, near St Meinrad; he had decided to build himself a primitive round house, in the style of an African hut. He thought of it as a place of retreat, a kind of monastery. When his daughter came to look at the site, she told him it was a place of corpses — a remark he dismissed until, when building began, a skeleton was uncovered, and Jung discovered that many French soldiers had died in the vicinity in 1799 when the Austrians blew up a bridge. Jung took this to indicate that his daughter had inherited some of the family's psychic powers.

Shortly before building began, Jung had a dream of a gigantic wolfhound bursting out of a primeval forest; Jung knew that the Wild Huntsman had commanded it to carry away a human soul. The next morning, he heard that his mother had died in the night. It was another glimpse of the 'invisible writing'.

The 'round house' at Bollingen developed into a two storey tower. It was primitive, without running water or electricity; but there was an element in Jung that craved the primitive. Over the years, the tower slowly developed into a fairly large house, complete with a meditation room for Jung. But his motives in building it were not entirely connected with asceticism; he and Toni Wolff often went there alone for weekends; Emma seems finally to have reconciled herself to the idea that her husband was a man who needed two wives and numerous mistresses.

For Jung, this period — in the early half of the twenties — was a time of spiritual search. He had already outgrown the ideas of *Psychological Types* by the time the book was published; but the ideas that would replace them were still in a state of chaos. The only book to emerge from this period, *The Psychology of the Unconscious* (published in 1926), is basically a brief summary, a backward look, at ground already covered, beginning with an account of Freud and psychoanalysis, continuing with an exposition of Adler's 'will to power' psychology, and concluding with an account of his own psychological types and the collective unconscious. On the subject of the archetypes, he is as unconvincing as he had been in 1912. He offers as an example Robert Mayer's discovery of the law of the conservation of energy, and finds various parallels in Buddhism and Polynesian religion, which lead him to assert that 'this idea has been stamped on the human brain for aeons' — to which a sceptic would retort that a similar argument could be used to prove that the bicycle and motor car are derived from the chariot of the sun in

Greek mythology and the chariot of Juggernaut of the Hindus.

Jung's solution to this state of intellectual suspension was to try to deepen the insights that had come to him through contact with North Africa — particularly the slowing down of time. If split-brain physiology had existed in 1924, Jung might have recognized that he was exploring the 'timeless' awareness of the right brain. As it was, he took the opportunity of a lecture trip to America in 1924 to visit the Pueblo Indians of Mexico. The North African trip had made him aware of how far his consciousness was conditioned by European civilization. He was among the Taos Indians at about the same time as D. H. Lawrence, and seems to have reached much the same conclusions as Lawrence. He quotes the Taos chief: 'See how cruel the whites look . . . Their eyes have a staring expression: they are always seeking something. What are they seeking?' Jung asked why he thought all whites were mad, and was told: 'They say that they think with their heads.' Jung asked what Indians thought with. 'Our hearts.'

Jung was impressed by the Indian conviction that certain ritual acts could influence the sun. It was, he noted, basically the same as the Christian idea that prayer can influence God. He was still struggling with the half-formulated insight that certain energies inside man can enter into harmony with the external world, bringing about strange signs and synchronicities.

In Mexico, he experienced another burst of 'active imagination.' He had a sensation as if a 'shapeless mist' was rising inside him, and this solidified into fantasies of Roman legions destroying cities in Gaul, St Augustine converting England, Charlemagne converting pagans by threat of death, crusaders burning and looting, and finally, Spanish conquistadors descending on the Aztecs with slaughter, fire and torture. It is, of course, the kind of fantasy that any historian might dream up; but Jung's abnormally active unconscious lent it reality. Arnold Toynbee once described how his own *Study of History* originated in a similar vision in Sparta; but for Toynbee, it was only a sudden overwhelming sense of the *reality* of the past. Jung's unconscious mind was showing him how to turn that reality into actual visions.

This enables us to grasp the most fundamental issue of all concerning Jung's work. It makes us aware that the real problem about the human mind is not its neuroses and psychoses, but its sheer *feebleness*. The violence of the Roman legions, the cruelty of the Spanish conquistadors, was something that *really happened*. Yet it is practically impossible for the human mind to *grasp* that it happened; compared to the present moment, it remains unreal, a kind of fairy story. *This* is what is wrong with human consciousness: that we are trapped in the present. Our minds can, potentially, conjure up other times and other places — it often happens when a certain odour, a certain old tune, a certain sensory impression, brings back the reality of the past so vividly that we want to burst into tears. Yet we cannot do it at will; consciousness seems as feeble as a baby's grip. Neurosis is due to this feebleness, the inability of the mind to throw off petty worries. When Jung discusses the sensory extravert type — the man who seems to feel that the present is the only reality — he is actually talking about all human beings.

Human evolution has been man's long, slow attempt to develop the power of the mind, to strengthen his mental 'grip', so he can *choose* his realities, instead of having to swallow whatever the present moment chooses to impose on him. And although Jung was no philosopher — no one can read his collected works without noticing that he spends much of his time going round in circles — he recognized the basic problem instinctively. He rejected Freud because Freud's essentially passive psychology leaves the human mind stuck in the present, with no hope of deliverance. He had an obscure but extremely powerful sense that the mind must learn to become active, to be capable of transforming everyday reality.

We cannot understand Jung's development in the mid-1920s unless we grasp that he was in the grip of a daemon that whispered that there *had* to be a solution to this problem. Freud's sexual theory, Adler's will to power theory, provided no answer. But neither, unfortunately, did Jung's own mythological theory. It was a step in the right direction, but no more than that.

This explains why, almost as soon as he was back in Zurich, he was once again on the move — this time to Africa. At that time, the theory of Dart and Leakey, that man originated in Africa, still lay a decade or more in the future; yet it is possible to believe that Jung knew it by a kind of second sight. He records that, visiting a game reserve in Nairobi, staring away to a distant horizon dotted with zebra, he suddenly felt 'This was the stillness of the eternal beginning.'

A similar recognition came to him when an old white man told him: 'This is not man's country, it's God's country. So if anything should happen, just sit down and don't worry.' Jung says: 'His words struck me as somehow significant . . . Evidently they represented the quintessence of his experience; not man but God was in command here — in other words, not will and intention, but inscrutable design.'

Inscrutable design. That was what Jung was looking for in Africa. It was what he had been looking for all his life: the sense that there is *meaning* outside us and around us: invisible writing. Here Jung could sense it. 'I enjoyed the "divine peace" of a still primeval country . . . Thousands of miles lay between me and Europe, mother of all demons. The demons could not reach me here — there were no telegrams, no telephone calls, no letters, no visitors. My liberated psychic forces poured blissfully back to the primeval expanses.' And the realization that grew from the experience of Africa was that 'within the soul from its primordial beginnings there has been a desire for light and an irrepressible urge to rise out of the primal darkness.' His vision of Africa seems to have been very close to that which Conrad expressed in *Heart of Darkness:* 'In reality a darkness altogether different from natural night broods over the land. It is the psychic primal night which is the same today as it has been for countless millions of years. The longing for light is the longing for consciousness.'

Yet Africa was not the solution of his problem. The problem was that his work was marking time — as became clear when *The Psychology of the Unconscious* appeared in 1926. What he had sought in Africa was that sense of the invisible world that lies around us. The primitive feels that he is surrounded by spirits. In Europe, poltergeist activity is regarded as an unexplainable manifestation of the unconscious; in Africa, it is regarded as a visible manifestation of invisible spirits. In a sense, an African would hardly be surprised to see an object floating across a room;

it would merely confirm what he knows to be true.

But what Jung wanted was more than a return to this primitive view of the world. He was reaching out towards an intuition that there can be a fruitful harmony between the mind and the powers of the universe. In ancient cultures, this tradition is known as magic, and Jung's thinking was becoming increasingly 'magical'. Yet he was not concerned with ritual or ceremonial magic — as W. B. Yeats was; he was concerned with the 'natural' magic of the unconscious: the 'magic', for example, that produces synchronicities. So in a sense, the African trip was a dead end rather than a beginning.

He had reached an impasse in another sense. In *Psychological Types*, it becomes very clear that Jung was deeply drawn to the early Church Fathers and to the Gnostics, with their strange philosophy of creation. Jung obviously felt that his psychology needed an extra dimension, and he hoped to find it in these sources. By 1926, when he returned from Africa, this hope had vanished. 'As far as I could see, the tradition that might have connected Gnosis with the present seemed to have been severed, and for a long time it proved impossible to find any bridge that led from Gnosticism — or neo-Platonism — to the contemporary world.' But the feeling of the necessity for such a bridge remained strong. And in 1928, a fragment of the solution was provided by his friend Richard Wilhelm, who sent him a translation of a Chinese mystical work called *The Secret of the Golden Flower*. This is, in fact, a curious combination of eastern mysticism and alchemy, symbolising the goal of meditation as the Elixir of Life. Jung was immediately struck to find that the book contained the mandala symbol. He was even more excited to find that the soul is symbolized both as a masculine cloud demon and as an earth-bound female white ghost; he saw these as symbols of the animus and anima — his own concept of the masculine soul that dwells in women and the feminine soul that dwells in men. (Brome quotes H. G. Wells as saying, after a meeting with Jung: 'I've always known I had a beautiful young girl trying to break out from inside me.') But perhaps the most exciting notion was that the aim of this spiritual alchemy was to produce an 'etheric body' known as the 'diamond body' — which corresponded very closely to Jung's concept of the self. One section began:

> If thou wouldst complete the diamond body with no
> outflowing,
> Diligently heat the roots of consciousness and life.
> Kindle light in the country close at hand,
> And there hidden, let thy true self always dwell.

That phrase 'with no outflowing' was obviously of
central importance; for the problem with neurotics — in
fact, with human beings in general — is a kind of *leakage* of
energy, due to fear, anxiety, general negativeness.

This was the reason that Gnosticism and early Christianity had always so appealed to Jung. For Freud, there are
only sick people and 'normal' people, who are like
everybody else. But Jung was far more interested in
supernormal people, in men like St Augustine and Goethe
and Nietzsche — in saints and supermen. Yet in a sense,
these are difficult to fit into a general picture of the human
mind — that is to say, into depth psychology. What Jung
wanted was a connection between the world of Gnosticism and early Christianity and the world of depth
psychology. *The Secret of the Golden Flower* suggested that
he might have found it — in alchemy.

Jung asked a Munich bookseller to locate for him some
books on alchemy. He also recollected that Herbert
Silberer, a friend of Vienna days, had written a book on
alchemy called *Problems of Mysticism and Its Symbolism*
(1917). Silberer, like Jung, had tried hard to expand the
rigid Freudian categories, for he felt that mystical experience is not merely a sublimation of sexuality. The book has
a strongly Jungian flavour, and this is undoubtedly why it
exasperated Freud to the point of breaking with Silberer.
Silberer fell into depression, and in 1923 committed
suicide by hanging himself from window bars — leaving a
torch shining on his face so his wife would see him as she
came in. (Freud seemed to have some frightening power
of inducing suicidal depression in 'heretics'; in 1919,
Viktor Tausk — another Freudian who had dared to think
for himself — committed suicide, while in early 1927, the
brilliant newcomer Wilhelm Reich had a nervous breakdown after Freud broke with him.) Jung had written
Silberer a warmly appreciative letter after reading *Problems*

of Mysticism, but it had failed to interest him in western alchemy — partly because Silberer had concentrated on later alchemical texts by writers like Hollandus and Philalethes that were even more obscure than the earlier ones.

The Munich bookseller found Jung a compilation called *Artis Auriferae* (1593), containing a number of classics of alchemy; but he found it incomprehensible, and pushed it aside in disgust. Two years later, he took it up again, and began making a glossary of basic alchemical terms. When it dawned on him that the alchemists were talking in symbols, he became increasingly fascinated. The problem began to obsess him. 'I worked along philological lines, as if I were trying to solve the riddle of an unknown language. In this way, the alchemical mode of expression gradually yielded up its meaning. It was a task that kept me absorbed for more than a decade.'

Anyone who has ever spent five minutes trying to read an alchemical text may fund Jung's obsession baffling and rather perverse. According to the alchemists, the Work begins by finding a substance called the *prima materia* (which some believe to be salt, some mercury, others earth of even water). This must be pulverized, mixed with a 'secret fire', and heated in a sealed vessel. This *prima materia* contains two elements, male and female, referred to as sol and luna, or sulphur and mercury. In the sealed vessel, these blacken and putrefy, a process known as the 'nigredo'. Then the mass should begin to show white flecks, and to turn white — a process known as the albedo. It becomes volatile, and recrystallizes as a white stone. In this stone, the male and female elements are united into a 'mysterium coniunctionis' or marriage, and it is capable of healing. At the next stage of the process, the white stone is added to 'mercury', and an obscure process known as 'exaltation' takes place. The stone turns green after being dissolved in acid — a stage known as the green lion — and finally turns .red. This is the Philosopher's Stone, which can turn base metals into gold, and which is also the Elixir of Life.

The most obvious explanation of all this is that the science of chemistry has existed for less than two hundred years. Its major figures — Priestley, Cavendish, Lavoisier, Dalton — were experimenting towards the end of the eighteenth century. Dalton announced his atomic theory in 1803. So we can dismiss talk about making gold out of other substances as sheer ignorance — the alchemists were unaware that gold is an element, and therefore cannot be 'made'.

But this explanation has failed to satisfy many acute minds. In the 1840s, a brilliant young lady named Mary Anne South (later Mrs Attwood) studied hypnosis, and became convinced that the Greeks had made use of hypnotic states in their Mysteries. She then wrote a book on alchemy, *A Suggestive Enquiry into the Hermetic Mystery* (1850) which suggested that alchemy itself was a coded form of the mystery religion of the ancients. When her father read the book, he was so shocked at the thought that she was revealing forbidden secrets to the mob that he bought up all available copies and burned them. W. Wynn Wescott, one of the founder members of the Order of the Golden Dawn — the magical society of which Yeats was a member — wrote a little book called *The Science of Alchymy*, which declared that all the chemical symbolism was a blind, and that alchemy was basically a mystery religion.

So Jung's 'discovery' about alchemy was, in a sense, a rediscovery of the ideas of Mrs Attwood and Wynn Wescott. Jung believed that alchemy is about the transmutation of the mind and the discovery of the self. Inevitably, he saw the male and female elements of the *prima materia* — the king and queen of alchemy — as the animus and anima; this seemed to indicate the alchemy is about psychological processes.

Jung's theory, briefly, is this. The alchemist regarded the Work with such intense seriousness that, quite unconsciously, he 'projected' his own desires and obsessions into it. 'While working on his chemical experiments the operator [alchemist] had certain psychic experiences which appeared to him as the particular behaviour of the chemical process. Since it was a question of projection, he was naturally unconscious of the fact that the experience had nothing to do with the matter . . . ' In other words, the alchemist 'saw' things in the process, rather as we might see faces in the fire. Jung cites a number of examples suggesting unconscious self-deception. One alchemist recommends taking rain water, and allowing consecrated red wine to fall into it drop by drop; the result, he says, will be a vision of creation as described in Genesis: first a kind of fog, then the emergence of light, and so on. Another described how, if seven pieces of metal bearing astrological symbols are heated in a crucible with a drop of the Philosopher's Stone, a flame of fire will fill the whole chamber and the starry firmament would appear overhead. Another says that during the Great Work, a 'wonderful variety of figures' — shapes of animals, reptiles and trees — will be seen in the crucible.

What is really happening, says Jung, is that the alchemist is unconsciously using active imagination, and therefore creating visions or hallucinations which invade his laboratory like waking dreams.

Readers of *Psychology and Alchemy* (1944) must have found all this baffling and rather unconvincing. Only the posthumous publication of the autobiography made it clear how Jung had arrived at this theory, and that he believed that the alchemists had undergone experiences similar to his own 'confrontation with the unconscious'. He comments, for example: 'One night I awoke and saw, bathed in bright light at the foot of my bed, the figure of Christ on the Cross. It was not quite life-size, but extremely distinct; and I saw that his body was made of greenish gold. The vision was marvellously beautiful, and yet I was profoundly shaken by it. A vision as such is nothing unusual for me, for I frequently see extremely vivid hypnagogic visions.'

So, according to Jung, alchemical texts, with their green lions and red dragons and starry firmaments, are actually descriptions of hypnagogic visions (visions seen between sleep and waking), which the alchemist believed to be a part of the chemical process.

For Jung, the next question was: what were the visions *about*? The answer is: religion. 'The soul possesses by nature a religious function', he says in *Psychology and Alchemy*. Western man has been spiritually starved by his materialistic, rationalistic civilization, and Christianity, with its tendency to dogmatism, has only made things worse. So the 'religious function' of the unconscious found its expression — through symbols, of course — in alchemy. Says Aniela Jaffé: 'Alchemy thus stood in a compensatory relationship to the world of consciousness and to Christianity, just as a dream does to the conscious situation of the dreamer.'

Which meant, in effect, that Jung could treat alchemy as one long, complicated dream, and employ his skill in dream interpretation. Alchemy, he believed, was basically a question of 'salvation' — or individuation, as he preferred to call it. It reflects Christianity in a kind of distorting mirror, but its images rise from even deeper within the psyche. (For Jung, the collective unconscious is deeper than the individual unconscious, and contains depths that can never be plumbed.) Instead of the Trinity of the Christians there is a quaternity — often reflected in mandala symbols divided into four parts. It is the prime task of education, says Jung, to convey the archetype of the God-image to the conscious mind. And the 'religious function' in the soul of the alchemists was trying to do precisely this. 'The archetypes of the unconscious can be shown empirically to be the equivalents of religious dogmas', so his attempt to interpret the 'dream' of alchemy became an attempt to plumb the depths of the collective unconscious.

The quest for the meaning of the alchemical dream occupied Jung through two large volumes, *Psychology and Alchemy* and *Mysterium Coniunctionis* — the latter his last completed book. These are among Jung's most important and fascinating works. Yet they raise in an even more acute form the question presented by *Symbols of Transformation* and *Psychological Types*: how far can this be regarded as an objective assessment of the subject, and how far is it merely a reflection of Jung's own incorrigible tendency to myth-making and intellectual maze-building? In an essay on 'The Nature of the Psyche', Jung admits that 'once [the unconscious] is admitted, one finds oneself at the mercy of all manner of hypotheses concerning this unconscious life, hypotheses that cannot be controlled by any observation.' And this goes to the heart of the problem. As Jung talks about the unconscious 'choosing' a certain type of myth in preference to another type, and explains that 'The son type does not call up a daughter as a complementary image from the depths of the "chthonic" unconscious — it calls up another son', even the most sympathetic reader feels inclined to believe that Jung could conjure up reasons for anything he wanted to prove. In a basic sense, Jung is still a Freudian: that is, he presents himself to us as the interpreter of the unconscious mind, wearing his wizard's robe and pointed hat, and the reader is expected to listen respectfully and nod in agreement. And sometimes the Freudianism is even closer to the surface, as when Jung explains that the king and queen are holding *left* hands because their union is incestuous, and 'incest symbolises union with one's own being, it means individuation or becoming the self'. Encountering passages like this tends to crystallize the reader's suspicion that Jung is reflecting his own obsessions and preoccupations, rather than those of the medieval alchemist, whose state of mind is inexpressibly remote from that of a modern Freudian psychologist.

At least one modern admirer of the Jungian doctrine of alchemy later came to reject it *in toto*. Francis Israel Regardie, at one time a member of the Order of the Golden Dawn, was studying alchemical tracts during a spell of illness in 1936 when he came upon Jung's commentary on the *Golden Flower*, and became convinced that this was the answer to the mystery. The result was a remarkable book called *The Philosopher's Stone*. But, unlike Jung, Regardie was also deeply versed in the magical tradition — he had been at one time secretary to Aleister Crowley — and he was also inclined to accept Mrs Attwood's theory that the alchemist could take on 'demiurgic powers' in a trance state. Jung, although versed in astrology and alchemy, never paid any serious attention to magic. Yet most of the great scientists of the late middle ages — for example, Cornelius Agrippa and Paracelsus — *were* 'magicians' as well as alchemists. And magicians believed that magical operations are performed with the aid of spirits. Jung actually believed in 'spirits', as we have seen, but his innate rationalism made it impossible for him to try to understand magic in terms of its own presuppositions. Regardie's book makes the reader aware that a whole dimension is missing from Jung's understanding of alchemy.

Oddly enough, Regardie later came to reject even the modified Jungianism of *The Philosopher's Stone*. In Salt Lake City, he encountered a modern alchemist, Albert Riedel, and witnessed experiments that left him in no doubt that alchemy is a chemical process, not a psycho-spiritual one, and that when Basil Valentinus tells the alchemist to take some antimony, pulverise it and place it in a retort, he means exactly what he says. In *Mysterium Coniunctionis*, Jung dismisses one of Gerhard Dorn's alchemical descriptions as a 'hair-raising chemical fantasy' — thereby begging once again the question he originally set out to answer: *why* the alchemist's descriptions are so bizarre and apparently meaningless.

The safest judgement on Jung's alchemical works is that they tell us a great deal about Jung and his basic ideas; how much they tell us about alchemy must remain an open question.

Six

The Sage of Küsnacht

For Jung, the 1930s provided a highly satisfactory period
of consolidation. He had become as much of a household
name as Freud. (When he went to the British Museum
Reading Room, and gave his name, the desk clerk asked:
'Not Freud, Jung and Adler?', and he replied: 'No, just
Jung'.) He had become one of the most respected citizens
of Zurich, as well known there as his grandfather had
been in Basle. He was surrounded by admiring disciples
(in Zurich, a female Jungian was known as a Jungfrau),
and received visitors and patients from all over the world.
One of his admirers, Frau Olga Froebe-Kapteyn, had built
a conference hall in the spacious grounds of her villa on
the shores of Lake Maggiore, the Casa Eranos, and from
1935 onwards, organized yearly conferences of noted
scholars and teachers; Jung became the central figure of
these conferences and virtually held court there. In 1933,
he was appointed President of the International Medical
Society for Psychotherapy; he also resumed academic
lectures, and in 1935 was appointed professor. In 1935 he
gave a highly successful series of lectures at the Tavistock
Clinic in London — his immense vitality and informal
manner made him a charismatic lecturer — and then went
on to Harvard; he returned to Harvard again in 1937. At
the invitation of the British government he travelled to
India in 1938, and was overpowered by its spell as he had
been overpowered by Africa.

Most important of all, his ideas were steadily develop-
ing; his 'analytical psychology' was becoming widely
accepted — or at least, widely known — as an alternative
to psychoanalysis. And with the discovery of alchemy, he
had annexed vast new intellectual territories, and provided himself with a fruitful field for investigation for the
rest of his life. His belief that the 'mysterious marriage' of

the alchemists was another name for individuation — the marriage of the conscious and unconscious — seemed one of the most exciting insights since Freud's discovery of the sexual theory in the 1890s. He was becoming increasingly certain that the 'religious function' is as natural and as important to man as the sexual function, and his theory of archetypes seemed to create an indissoluble link between religion and psychology. Archetypes were defined as the basic patterns of the collective unconscious, a kind of instinctive way of knowing, just as instincts are an inborn way of acting; Jung continued to find evidence for them in all the world's religions. His admirers felt that Jung was creating one of the boldest and most comprehensive intellectual syntheses in world history; and in spite of a certain outward modesty, Jung was possessed by much the same conviction.

There was, it must be acknowledged, a negative side to Jung's character. In spite of increasing recognition, he felt that his ideas were insufficiently acknowledged, and he could be thin-skinned about it. When an essay he wrote on Joyce's *Ulysses* was turned down as being too hostile, he at first tried to insist on its publication, evidently stung by the rejection. When a student sent him a review that questioned his scientific attitude, Jung became pompous: 'Supposing that my attitude really does exhibit such easily recognisable faults, how do you square this with the fact that I unite at least seven honorary doctorates . . . I am, by your leave, an honorary member of the Academy of German Scientists and Physicians, a Fellow of the Royal Society . . . '; and he goes on to list his 'qualifications'. In 1944, the discovery that a review of *Psychology and Alchemy* had been shortened drew the embittered comment: 'This is yet another reminder of the fact that I have to be presented to my contemporaries only as a third class passenger . . . ' When crossed, he had an explosive temper, and was liable to nagging and carping. He had many traits of what Freud called the 'anal erotic' — obsessively punctual, tidy and formal. Aniela Jaffé, later his secretary, remarked: 'Every typing mistake was re-proachfully and copiously commented on.' A mistake could lead to grumbling for the rest of the day. All this indicates unmistakably that this sage who talked about individuation and profound religious experience was himself by no means an integrated personality. Like a spoilt child who has been given his way too often, he was the victim of his own negative emotions. Towards the end of his life, he was to admit: 'The older I become, the less [I realize] I have understood or had insight into or known about myself'. An example is provided by some comments he made about Kierkegaard in a letter of 1943: 'To such [biased] people his problems and his grizzling are entirely acceptable, because to them it serves the same purpose as it served him: you can then settle everything in the study and need not do it in life. Out there things are apt to get unpleasant.' Jung seemed quite unaware that he was also inclined to 'settle things in his study' and make no real attempt at self-discipline.

All this helps to explain why the coming of the Second World War plunged Jung into depression. He had become accustomed to the busy life of the famous man; now, suddenly, the streets of Zurich were almost devoid of traffic, food was in short supply, and Jung found himself in an isolation that was a little like premature retirement. His attitude towards the modern world was becoming increasingly negative; he loathed its art, its music, its literature, its politics. He wrote gloomily in a letter: 'Why in hell is man unable to grow up? The Lord of this world is certainly the Devil.' His contemporary H. G. Wells had experienced a similar reaction to this spectacle of violence, and changed from a Utopian optimist to an embittered pessimist almost overnight. But then, Wells had always been a scientific materialist. Jung, with his religious preoccupations, should in theory have been less vulnerable.

What was happening suggests that there was something missing in Jung's psychology. He was certainly not sexually frustrated, and he had no 'religious problems' (he once said that most patients over the age of thirty-five had religious problems). Yet he was allowing himself to slip into a thoroughly negative attitude towards himself and towards the world. The real problem was simply lack of motivation, lack of projects to excite his enthusiasm — leading, in turn, to loss of what Janet called 'psychological tension'. Jung's psychology, with its collective unconscious and archetypes, its animus and anima and shadow and enantiodromia, was too complex to grasp such a simple problem.

The accident of January 1944 — described at the opening of this book — and the heart attack that followed, seem inevitable consequences of the depression and pessimism of the war years. They might almost have been engineered by his own unconscious mind, for — as we have seen — the result was a startling self-renewal. Jung had surrendered to his rational self and all its rational negations and dislikes. Now suddenly, the rational self collapsed, and he once again became aware of the 'numinous'. 'It was as if I were in an ecstasy. I felt as though I were floating in space, as though I were safe in the womb of the universe — in a tremendous void, but filled with the highest possible feeling of happiness'.

This was an important step beyond the 'confrontation with the unconscious' of the First World War. 'I would not have imagined that any such experience was possible. It was not a product of imagination. The visions and experiences were utterly real; there was nothing subjective about them'. The visions of Elijah and Salome and Philemon *had* been imagination — albeit 'active imagination'. They had convinced Jung that the mind can create its own reality, in defiance of the physical world. But these 'visions' *were* real; so they spoke of a reality *outside* himself. For ten years or more he had been writing about this reality — the reality underlying religious and mystical experience; now he knew it at first hand. Interestingly enough, he emphasizes its timeless element. 'We shy away from the word "eternal", but I can describe the experience only as the ecstasy of a non-temporal state in which present, past and future are one. Everything that happens in time had been brought together into a concrete whole. Nothing was distributed over time, nothing could be measured by temporal concepts.' It was as if Jung's consciousness had been transferred to the timeless realm of the right brain. And if 'individuation' means that left and right brain consciousness have ceased to be divided, then Jung had finally achieved a degree of individuation.

The negativeness of the war years also evaporated. 'Something else, too, came to me from my illness. I might formulate it as an affirmation of things as they are: an unconditional "yes" to that which is, without subjective protests . . . ' And he adds the penetrating comment: 'At the beginning of the illness, I had the feeling that there was something wrong with my attitude, and that I was to some extent responsible for the mishap.'

This was perhaps the major watershed in Jung's life. Ever since he had entered the Burghölzli, he had been battling for 'primacy', for success, for dominance, for fame — no doubt spurred unconsciously by the memory of his father's pathetic failure. Jung had come on the scene at an important point in European intellectual history, when various forms of scientific reductionism were becoming an 'unshakeable dogma'. Jung had sensed that his life's purpose would be to fight to undermine such reductionism, if only to chip a few small fragments from its foundations. And this is why it was so important to him to be accepted as a scientist; it explains why he fiercely repudiated the slightest suggestion that some of his attitudes might be closer to those of the artist or imaginative creator. In the letter in which he lists his 'scientific' qualifications, he also denies that he is a romantic. Yet in retrospect, nothing could be plainer than that this is precisely what he is.

The encounter with death seems to have made him aware that it was unnecessary to keep up the frantic pretence that he was a scientist and nothing but. There were, as we have seen, no immediate and obvious results; he did not suddenly announce any sort of 'conversion'. The first sign of the more relaxed attitude was the postscript, in 1948, to the earlier article on belief in spirits, in which he admitted that his previous views were inadequate. But an introduction on 'Psychology and Spiritualism' (to Stewart White's *Unobstructed Universe*) still insists that the book can be read merely as an interesting manifestation of the unconscious. It was another two years before he told frankly the story of the ghost that had haunted the cottage he had stayed in after the First World War. But he still made no mention of the experiments that he and Bleuler had performed with the Austrian medium Rudi Schneider in the 1920s — experiments in which he had witnessed 'materializations and psychokinesis (or movement of objects).It was for Aniela Jaffé to reveal these after Jung's death, in an essay in which she merely says 'Jung never utilised these experiments scientifically' — meaning that he chose not to admit to them.

In a sense, all this was relatively unimportant compared to Jung's preface to the Wilhelm translation of the *I Ching*, in which he finally acknowledges that he had been taking the Chinese oracle seriously for many years. In the same year (1950) he also wrote the first short essay 'On Synchronicity', delivered as a lecture to a sympathetic audience at Eranos the following year. The most striking thing about this lecture is not that Jung has decided to break with his lifelong rationalism by formulating an 'acausal connecting principle', but that he still goes to such lengths to try to disguise what he is doing. He begins by defining synchronicity as 'meaningful coincidence', and gives an example from his own experience: how in 1949 he had made a note of an inscription about a creature that was half man and half fish. There was fish for lunch; someone mentioned a custom of making 'April fish'; a former patient showed him pictures of fish; he was shown an embroidery with sea monsters and fishes; finally, a patient dreamed of fish in the night. A few months later, immediately after writing this down, he found a large fish on the wall by the lake. Yet having described all this, he explains that, on consideration, he has decided that this was a 'chance grouping'. So before the discussion is properly launched he has already offered an example of synchronicity, then taken it back.

He now goes on to describe how a student friend had a dream of a Spanish city, and when he went to Spain on holiday soon after, recognized the scene of his dream, even to a carriage with two cream-coloured horses. *This* is plainly not synchronicity, but precognition. Then he goes on to describe some of Rhine's experiments in card-guessing; but this is obviously 'ESP' (extra-sensory perception) and not synchronicity. The first example of 'genuine synchronicity' concerns an intellectual woman patient whose rigid rationalism frustrated his efforts at psychoanalysis. One day after she had been recounting a dream about a golden scarab, there was a knocking at the window pane; when Jung opened it, a golden-green scarab beetle flew in. The 'coincidence' punctured the patient's rationalism and Jung was able to proceed more satisfactorily. But now, having finally committed himself to an instance of synchronicity, Jung again swiftly confuses the issue by mentioning more examples of ESP and precognition, as well as telepathy. He then turns to astrology, and describes an experiment in which he analysed 180 marriages statistically to see whether the old astrological belief that married couples have certain conjunctions and oppositions in common has any factual foundation. The figures showed that there *were* many such conjunctions, and that the number was well above chance. This again, says Jung, must be synchronicity — when any astrologer would tell him that it is, on the contrary, the result of some unknown physical law that connects the magnetic forces of the earth with those of the planets.

So at the end of the lecture, we are left in a state of confusion, having been offered only one 'genuine' example of synchronicity, and a dozen or so examples of ESP, precognition, telepathy, etc. By surrounding the case of the scarab with so much irrelevant material, Jung makes it hard to see what conclusion he draws from it.

But in the short book he based on the lecture, *Synchronicity, An Acausal Connecting Principle* (1952), he is willing to go a little further. Here he resorts to his old technique of blinding the reader with science — or at least, with classical learning and philosophy. But once he has erected the scientific and philosophical smokescreen, he is prepared to lay some of his cards on the table. He cites, for example, Camille Flammarion's case of M. Fortgibu and the plum pudding. A certain M. Deschamps was given a piece of plum pudding by M. Fortgibu when he was a boy in Orléans. Ten years later, he saw some plum pudding in a Paris restaurant and asked if he could have some — only to be told that it had been ordered by the same M. Fortgibu. Many years later he was invited to a meal that included plum pudding, and remarked that all that was wanting was M. Fortgibu. At that moment, the door opened, and in walked a doddering and senile M. Fortgibu, who had come to the wrong address . . .

Later in the chapter, he quotes Albertus Magnus — one of the fathers of western magic — to the effect that 'a certain power to alter things indwells in the human soul and subordinates the other things to her, particularly when she is swept into a great excess of love or hate or the like'. At last, then, he is willing to admit that synchronicity and magic are much the same thing. At this point, he once more beats a retreat, and speaks about the *I Ching* and the

Chinese concept of Tao, which he translates as 'meaning'. Then follows a lengthy account of the astrological experiment, with tables and graphs, and admissions that some of his previous figures were wrong. This is followed by an erudite chapter on various forerunners of the idea of synchronicity: Hippocrates, Pico della Mirandola, Agrippa, Paracelsus, Kepler and Leibniz. This chapter brings us to the conclusion of the book — and the reader still has the feeling that he has missed some essential link in the chain of logic.

The conclusion, in fact, is no more satisfactory than the early chapters, for it is mainly devoted to the question of psycho-physical parallelism, or the relation between the soul and the body, using this as an analogy for the relation between physical and psychic events. It contains, in the midst of a long paragraph, the all-important sentence: 'either there are physical processes which cause psychic happenings, or there is a pre-existent psyche which organises matter'. That is to say, the mind can, in some way, 'make things happen'. Yet he seems to have denied this in an earlier chapter, where he discusses such examples as the patient with the scarab, and concludes that her dream of a scarab was some sort of precognition that a scarab would bang on the window the next day. Jung seems to be giving with one hand and taking back with the other.

But in this final chapter, he cites a case that seems to offer a key to the mystery. He describes how a woman patient almost died after a difficult birth, and found herself in the air above her body, looking down on it. She could see that the doctor was slightly hysterical; then her family came in, and she observed their reactions. Behind her, she knew — although she could not see — there was a marvellous, park-like landscape with spring flowers, which she knew to be the entrance to 'the other world'. She knew that if she looked at it, she might be tempted not to re-enter her body, so she kept her eyes in the other direction. When she woke up, she was able to describe to the nurse what she had seen, and the nurse was obliged to admit that the patient was correct about the doctor and other matters.

This, says Jung, seems to demonstrate that there are perceptions independent of the body, and of space and time, and 'where sense perceptions are impossible from the start, it can hardly be an example of anything but synchronicity'. The reader blinks with astonishment, wondering what an 'out-of-the-body experience' has to do with synchronicity. Yet it must be admitted that, in spite of Jung's obvious reluctance to be too explicit, his general drift is perfectly clear. His own near-death experience of 1944 had convinced him that the psyche is independent of the body, which seems to imply the reality of life after death. In fact, in an essay on 'The Soul and Death', written in 1934, he had come close to affirming the same thing, commenting that all the world's major religions seem to accept that life is a preparation for 'the ultimate goal of death'. (Even here he has deliberately worded it so that no one can accuse him of believing in life *after* death.) Such out-of-the-body experiences, taken together with 'meaningful coincidences', certainly suggest that the universe is not a Chaotic conglomeration of matter. We are somehow involved in a profoundly meaningful process, *and can influence that process*. So synchronicities may be understood in two ways: either as a 'magical' process — an influence exerted by the unconscious mind upon the world around us — or as a kind of nudge from some unknown guardian angel, whose purpose is to tell us that life is not as meaningless as it looks.

Yet all this is dressed up in talk about causality and non-causality, statistics and experiments, Greek and Chinese modes of thought, that are designed to give it the appearance of a scientific hypothesis. So is the sentence in the first chapter: 'One of the most problematic and momentous centuries the world has ever known separates us from that still mediaevalistic age when the philosophizing mind believed it could make assertions beyond what could be empirically proved' — implying that he, Dr Jung, would not dream of making any such assertions. Yet this sentence follows a section in which he acknowledges Schopenhauer as the 'godfather' of his idea of synchronicity — Schopenhauer, one of the first great loves of Jung's romantic youth. In a sense, Jung has now come full circle. He has returned to an affirmation of the romantic and poetic ideals of his mid-teens. But he does it with extreme caution, afraid of losing the ground gained by a lifetime of scientific investigation — or perhaps merely of losing face.

The same ambivalence is apparent in another of the most

controversial works of the 1950s: *Flying Saucers: A Modern Myth of Things Seen in the Skies* (1958). Jung's theory is that flying saucers are 'projections' from the collective unconscious. He sees as their chief significance the fact that they are circular — like mandalas. They are, then, a 'projection' of our unconscious craving for a saviour — or, what amounts to the same thing, for individuation. (The mandala is the symbol of God *and* the Self.)

But there is a complication; Jung admits that UFOs can be photographed and cause images on radar screens. Then how *can* they be 'projections'? — for we may recall that projection means basically a vision or hallucination. Jung leaves that question unanswered; but the answer is clearly implied. Under certain conditions, a 'projection' *can* cause physical effects. The mind can affect physical reality. But Jung is careful not to underline this aspect, and few of the commentaries on his book even mention it.

But one further complication is provided by an interview between Jung and the aviator Charles Lindbergh in the summer of 1959. 'To my astonishment', said Lindbergh (in a letter to his publisher's wife) 'I found that Jung accepted flying saucers as factual. On the one hand, he didn't seem in the least interested in psychological aspects. On the other, he didn't seem at all interested in factual information relating to the investigation of flying saucer reports.' When Lindbergh told Jung that the US Air Force had found no evidence whatever for flying saucers, 'it was obvious that he did not wish to pursue the subject further'. Lindbergh persisted, pouring cold water on the sightings, and quoting his friend General Spaatz (of the US Air Force) as saying: 'Don't you suppose that if there was anything true about this flying saucer business, you and I would have heard about it by this time?' Jung's reply was: 'There are a great many things going on around this earth that you and General Spaatz don't know about.'* It seems clear, then, that once again Jung was telling slightly less than he knew — or believed — when presenting his views to the public. Significantly, Lindbergh commented: 'One intuitively feels

---

* *C. G. Jung Speaking,* edited by William McGuire and R. C. F. Hull. p.364. I have also been told that, after Jung's death, his niece was quoted as saying that he accepted flying saucers as physically real.

the elements of mysticism and greatness about him — even
though they may have been mixed, at times, with elements
of charlatanism.'

The same caution, the determination not to sacrifice his
status as a scientist, can be observed in Jung's attitude
towards religion in the final decade of his life. He produced
two major works on this subject, *Aion* (1951) and *Answer to
Job* (1952), the second of which caused more controversy
than any book he had ever written. *Aion* is a work of
considerable obscurity, even by Jung's standards: it is
centrally an analysis of the significance of the Christ figure.
Concealed in the midst of its discussion of psychological
and religious symbolism is a startling thesis. Jung believes
that Christianity arose as a deep necessity of the collective
unconscious. Man was sick of paganism and of Rome;
something deeper, more spiritually satisfying, had to take
its place. Jung also believes that the change had to occur
when it did, two thousand years ago, at the beginning of
the Age of Pisces — and it is significant that the symbol of
Christianity is the fish. In short, *Aion* is an attempt to
describe human history as the unfolding of a necessary
process, originating in the collective unconscious. The
inner compulsion of the book is close to that of the opening
sections of *Psychological Types*, dealing with Tertullian,
Origen and the early Church. But in trying to show the
psychological necessity of Christianity, Jung was going
further than in any previous work. He was, in effect,
staking his claim as a philosopher of history, together with
Spengler and Toynbee. It could be regarded as his final
'answer to Freud', his fullest analysis of the 'religious
function' of the soul. Nevertheless, he was careful to guard
his flank. In an interview with Mircea Eliade at the Eranos
Conference in 1952, shortly after the publication of *Aion*, he
states: 'I am and remain a psychologist. I am not interested
in anything that transcends the psychological content of
human experience. I do not even ask myself whether such
transcendence is possible . . . ' This would have rung false
even in 1912, after the publication of *Symbols of Transformation*, in which it is obvious that Jung experiences powerful
emotional involvement with St Augustine and Christian
symbolism; in *Psychological Types* it has become self-
evident. Jung's aim had always been to widen the categories of Freudianism, to insist that religion is as important for

the unconscious as sex. *Aion* is an assertion of man's basic craving for 'transcendence'. So his insistence that 'I do not even ask myself whether such transcendence is possible' must be regarded as another attempt to take back with one hand what he has given with the other.

Answer to Job succeeds in being even more ambiguous. In his autobiography, Jung explains: 'The many questions from the public and from patients had made me feel that I must express myself more clearly about the religious problems of modern man. For years I had hesitated to do so, because I was fully aware of the storm I would be unleashing. But at last I could not help being gripped by the problem, in all its urgency and difficulty, and I found myself compelled to give an answer.'

Anyone who takes this to mean that Jung intends to make an unambiguous statement of his own religious beliefs is due for a disappointment. *Answer to Job* is as obscure as anything Jung ever wrote. The question being posed is, of course, that of the existence of evil. Dostoevsky had dealt with this in the 'Grand Inquisitor' chapter of *The Brothers Karamazov*, and Wells had made it the subject of the most powerful of all his novels, *The Undying Fire*, a modern version of the story of Job. Jung's controversial answer is that God cannot be wholly good — he contains a dark side. He goes on to discuss the story of Job, and concludes that Job scored a moral victory over Jehovah. This somehow necessitated the birth of Christ, for in Christianity the problem of evil is finally brought out into the open. The Virgin Mary is also important as a symbol of redemption. But in contrast to these wholly good figures, the figure of the Antichrist, Satan, becomes increasingly important. Satan is God's 'shadow', and the fact that the Supreme Being can have a 'shadow' indicates that God may not be the ultimately omnipotent being he is supposed to be. (This seems to have been the aspect of the book that caused so much controversy.) Christianity has remained unsatisfactory because Jesus is wholly good, and offers himself as a kind of hostage for human evil.

Jung's answer is contained in his idea of individuation. The opposites — conscious and unconscious — must come to terms, learn to understand one another, to cooperate. Only then will conflict (neurosis) be transcended. Jung sees the coming of the Age of Aquarius as the new synthesis; the

mandala has emerged as its typical symbol, a new whole-
ness. So the answer to the problem of evil lies in Jungian
psychology and its concept of individuation.

Jung does not, of course, dot the i's and cross the t's as
vigorously as this. Nevertheless, it is clearly implied.
Hence the storm raised by the book among theologians — a
storm which made it the only book by Jung to appear on the
American bestseller lists. In effect, Jung was setting himself
up as the prophet of the new era, its John the Baptist. And,
in a sense, his claim was more reasonable than it sounds.
He wrote in a letter: 'We stand in much greater need of a
widening of our reflective consciousness, so that we can be
more clearly aware of the opposing forces within us, and
cease trying to sweep evil out of the way, or denying it or
projecting it, as we have done until now.' Jung is merely
restating, in a more complex way, Bernard Shaw's assertion that God is himself incomplete, and that man's
business is to try to complete him by attaining wider
consciousness and deeper self-knowledge. But Jung went
one step further than Shaw. He believed that healing
tendencies are welling up from the depths of the unconscious mind, and that, therefore, man stands on the
threshold of a new stage in his evolution. In that sense, the
Answer to Job, for all its obscurity and ambiguity, is the
capstone of the structure he had been creating all his life. It
is his ultimate repudiation of 'reductionism'. In fact, in his
assertion that the dogma of the Assumption of the Virgin
Mary (made by the Church in 1950) is the most significant
religious event since the Reformation, he seems to be
echoing Goethe's view that 'the eternal feminine draws us
upward and on'. The *Answer to Job* could be seen as his own
equivalent of the second part of *Faust*.

Answer to Job was written as a result of a period of illness.
Jung's constitution had always been magnificent, but
during the last ten years of his life he was troubled
constantly by minor illness. In 1952, Toni Wolff died, at the
age of sixty-three; Jung did not attend her funeral. They
had drawn apart in recent years. Ruth Bailey, an English-
woman whom Jung had met in Africa — and who became
the companion of Jung's last years — quotes Jung as saying
'Toni is coming today — I hope she doesn't stay very long'.

Jung was a very heavy smoker, which caused bursts of
rapid pulse movement. His chief relaxation was reading

detective stories — anything from Simenon to Agatha Christie. And although he was working on his final book, *Mysterium Coniunctionis*, until 1955, he seems to have felt — as Ruth Bailey said — 'that he had said everything it had been given him to say'. Ruth Bailey found him demanding and querulous, something of a spoilt child. When she arrived after the death of Emma, in November 1955, Jung told her: 'I am a man who can get into great rages. Take no notice of them'. But when he nagged her all morning about two tomatoes, she had to threaten to leave to make him calm down. He then told her, with the unconscious egoism of a man who has always had his own way: 'All you have to remember is not to make me angry'.

Fortunately, there was still work to be done. In 1956, his publisher Kurt Wolff persuaded him to work on his autobiography, and he began — in collaboration with Aniéla Jaffé — in 1957, in his eighty-second year. He had always been curiously reticent about his private life, perhaps anxious that not too much should be known about his relations with women. But when he had set down his memories of childhood, he began to work with enthusiasm. For the first time, he described his breakdown of 1913 and his 'confrontation with the unconscious', enabling readers to understand what he meant by a 'projection'. He also spoke openly about his 'psychic' experiences — telepathy, poltergeists, precognitive dreams — so that it became clear, again for the first time, why he so decisively rejected Freud's anti-occultism. *Memories, Dreams, Reflections* made it very clear that Jung's life had been a version of the quest that had driven so many romantics, from Goethe to Yeats. But for readers of his other books, it also made clear something he had so far been determined to keep hidden: that the scientific psychologist was a public image and, to some extent, a deliberate deception. For many readers, it was almost as startling as discovering, let us say, that an eminent moralist and family man was actually a homosexual or paedophile. Yet in the long run, it did nothing but good; it allowed many readers to find their way into his major works without being baffled and frustrated by the many obstructions he had deliberately set up to disguise his passionate subjectivity.

In 1959 he was interviewed for BBC television by the journalist John Freeman. Subsequently, a British publisher asked Freeman to try to persuade Jung to collaborate on a popular book about his work. Jung demurred — again obviously worried about his scientist image — until he had a dream in which he was addressing a vast crowd of people. Thereafter, he worked to the point of exhaustion on a long essay 'Approaching the Unconscious'. It spoke of the slow evolution of human consciousness, of the 'split' that grew up between conscious and unconscious as a result of this evolution, and ended with a section called 'Healing the Split', which contains what is virtually a statement of faith:

> In a period of human history when all available energy is spent in the investigation of nature, very little attention is paid to the essence of man, which is his psyche, although many resear- ches are made into its conscious functions. But the really complex and unfamiliar part of the mind, from which symbols are produced, is still virtually unexplored. It seems almost incredible that though we receive signals from it every night, deciphering these communications seems too tedious for any but a few people to be bothered with it. Man's greatest instrument, his psyche, is little thought of, and is often mistrusted and despised. 'It's only psychological' too often means: It is nothing . . .
>
> This modern standpoint is surely one-sided and unjust. It does not even accord with the known facts. Our actual knowledge of the unconscious shows that it is a natural phenomenon, and that, like Nature herself, it is at least *neutral*. It contains all aspects of human nature — light and dark, beautiful and ugly, good and evil, profound and silly. The study of individual, as well as of collective, symbolism is an enormous task, and one that has not yet been mastered. But a beginning has been made at last. The early results are encouraging, and they seem to indicate an answer to many so far unanswered questions of present-day mankind.

Jung meant, of course: 'I have made a beginning at last, and my results indicate an answer to the unanswered questions of mankind . . . ' He had no possible doubt that his life-work had thrown a searchlight beam into the innermost recesses of human nature, and answered the question of why man is alive. It was therefore fitting that, ten days after writing these words, Jung should have taken to his bed with his final illness. The pessimism that had made him tell Laurens Van der Post 'I am an increasingly lonely old man writing for other lonely men' led him to write a querulous letter to a friend, Dr Michael Fordham, declaring that nobody understood him and that his work had been a failure. Fordham found Jung in his dressing gown, wearing a skull cap, and his conversation was confused and distressed. After a silence he said: 'You had better go.' Soon after, on 17 May 1961, a brain embolism made his speech blurred. On 6 June 1961, he said to Ruth Bailey: 'Let's have a really good red wine tonight', and sent her off to the cellar. Soon after, he relapsed into a coma, and died in the afternoon. In retrospect, we may feel that his last words were as appropriate as Goethe's: 'More light'.

Seven

Doubts and Reservations

While I have attempted to refrain from critical comment on Jung's ideas and attitude, it has probably become plain in the course of this book that I have a number of reservations about him. Anthony Storr confesses in the postscript to his own book on Jung: 'It is easy to lose patience with Jung, as I have myself at times'. He goes on to find fault with Jung's preoccupation with the occult, but says that he finds a great deal in Jung's psychology 'profoundly valuable'. I personally have no quarrel whatever with Jung's occultism, since it was all based on personal experience; but I feel extremely dubious about some of his purely psychological theories.

To describe Jung as a romantic is not, of course, in itself a criticism. A romantic is basically a person who feels that the world is full of hidden meanings — that discovery and adventure lie around every corner. This seems to me a broader, and therefore truer, attitude than that of the pessimist who feels that human life is short, brutal and pointless. The romantic recognizes that the problem lies in our own limitations, in the narrowness of our senses. So when a romantic also happens to be a realist, he is likely to devote a great deal of his life to a search for meaning — which is synonymous with self-transformation. Jung was such a person; the result is a remarkable body of work that can bear comparison with the *oeuvre* of any of the major figures of the nineteenth century.

But when a romantic denies strenuously that he *is* a romantic, the result is likely to be certain inner contradictions. Hegel, for example, tries to present his 'system' as if it sprang out of pure reason and logic; so he flings up a dense verbal smokescreen to make it sound academically respectable. Jung is seldom as obscure as Hegel, but the parallel holds good. Whenever he wishes to speak about something that touches his deepest convictions, he clears his throat and says: 'Speaking purely as a psychologist . . .' Storr points out that Freud has a great advantage over Jung because he writes so clearly and simply, as if he has nothing to hide. By comparison, Jung often seems to be trying to blind the reader with science.

Let us look more closely at Jung's development of the idea of the unconscious.

We have seen that, in the modern sense of the word, the notion was virtually invented by Freud. Freud had been studying with Charcot in Paris, and observed Charcot's remarkable demonstration of hypnosis. A person under hypnosis could be told, for example, that ten minutes after awakening, he would remove one of his shoes and place it on the table. In due course he would do this; and if asked why he had done it, would give some perfectly reasonable explanation. Clearly, the subject of the experiment was *two persons*, one of whom knew nothing about the other. And this could explain how a patient like the famous 'Anna O' could break off a conversation, climb a tree, come down again, and look astonished if the doctor asked her why she had climbed the tree, having no memory of her action. Freud concluded that the unconscious mind is far more powerful than the conscious mind, and that we are always doing things without really understanding their true motivations. Observation of his patients' 'transferences' to himself convinced Freud that the hidden motive is always sex. In Vienna around 1900, when sex was something respectable people never mentioned, this seemed highly plausible.

The problem with Freud's vision of man is that it is essentially *passive*. We are mere puppets in the hands of our unconscious minds. The surface of the mind may look calm enough, like a peaceful stretch of countryside with farms and orchards; under the surface there are tremendous forces that can produce earthquakes and volcanic eruptions.

Jung accepted this notion without question. But he was a romantic optimist by temperament, a man who regarded the universe as an exciting mystery into which, with luck, the poet and the scientist can obtain a few basic insights. So his line of attack on Freudian pessimism and 'reductionism' would have to begin from the notion that the mysterious underground forces are not as dangerous and menacing as Freud believed. He was the son of a clergyman, and his interest in St Augustine and the early Church Fathers reveals that he believed that the experience of God and religion could not be reduced to disguised sexual impulses. He was a lover of literature, and he certainly did not believe that the states of mind induced by poetry are mere 'escapism'. His problem was to rescue these from Freud. We have seen that it was his reading of a book on mythology that gave him the idea of how this could be done. He invented a still deeper layer of the unconscious, containing the basic myths of mankind. To modern ears, this does not sound implausible. We know, for example, that certain finches were bred for generations on the Galapagos Islands, where they never saw a predator. But when their descendants were taken back to California, they reacted with instant alarm at the sight of a hawk. Obviously, the image of a hawk was somehow encoded in their genes — or, as Jung would say, in the collective unconscious of the finch species. So why not similar images of heroes, gods, demons and so on in the human mind? The answer is: because it is hard to see any need for them. It mattered to the finch's survival to recognize a hawk. It is hard to see what difference it could make to a human being to think that the wind comes from a tube that hangs down from the sun . . .

This is not, of course, to flatly deny Jung's idea of the archetypes. They may well be a reality. But we should understand clearly how Jung came to *decide* they existed. He had accepted the Freudian view of the unconscious as a vast and mysterious underground realm. So it was natural for him to extend the image, and to imagine descending deeper still, to depths on which *he* could stake his claim. It is significant that so many of Jung's dreams, from the childhood dream of the phallus on the throne, involve descending into a kind of underworld. And from Jung's 'discovery' of the collective unconscious, his life-task was clear and obvious: to try to map out something of its geography, and to try to find proofs of its existence in mythology and religion. Alchemy was ideal for his purpose, for its baffling documents can be interpreted like dreams. Jung believed that he was proceeding scientifically, but most Freudians remain convinced that he was inventing his own underground realm, rather as Tolkein invented Middle Earth. There is at least an element of truth in this view.

Now before Freud, the picture of the human psyche was simpler. The view implicit in the work of Janet, for example, is that a human being could be compared to an automobile, whose ego is the driver, and whose 'mind' is the engine hidden under the bonnet. But the fact that it is 'hidden' does not make it 'unconscious'. It is at most 'subconscious' — lying just below consciousness. And just as a driver can find out a great deal about the engine by raising the bonnet, or simply observing closely what happens when he brakes, accelerates and changes gear, so human beings can learn a great deal about the workings of their own minds by introspection.

Of course, there are certain parts of the mind that could be called 'unconscious'. My brain contains every memory I have accumulated since birth, and this library is so enormous that we could never hope to bring it all back to consciousness. But there is nothing particularly mysterious about memory. I might, for example, go into a physics laboratory, and be shown the computer in which all the data of all past experiments is stored. I would not call this the 'unconscious mind' of the laboratory. And if there was another computer containing the results of experiments from all over the world, I would certainly not call it the collective unconscious. They are only computers.

How does neurosis arise? From childhood on, we are subjected to all kinds of fears and dangers. Some are real, some we imagine or exaggerate. Someone might tell me a shocking story about cruelty that engenders a permanently 'nasty feeling' about old houses or overgrown gardens. A bold, cheerful person will explore the world and realize that many of the fears were unwarranted. A timid, shy person may go through life with many childish fears and anxieties still unexorcized. He (or she) will be more likely to become subject to neurosis than the bolder spirit.

According to Janet, the basic condition for neurosis is the *abaissement du niveau mental*, or lowering of the mind threshold — a phrase, incidentally, that Jung used throughout his life (so often, indeed, that there is a long entry devoted to it in the index of his collected works). We may recall that Janet believed psychological health to be a matter of 'psychological tension', a sense of motivation and purpose. If this is lowered, by boredom or illness or depression, it constitutes an *abaissement du niveau mental*, and the person may become a prey to fears and anxieties that would have seemed absurd when he felt healthier. We experience a lowering of our mental threshold during the night, and we are all familiar with the experience of waking in the early hours of the morning and beginning to worry about all kinds of things. This is a simple model of Janet's view of how neurosis works. Then there are further stages — a narrowing of attention, which leads to a sense of monotony and a still further lowering of the mental threshold. There is a 'vicious circle' effect.

Fundamentally, our problem as living creatures is to adjust to life, and, if possible, to 'get on top of it'. We do this when we have a sense of purpose and motivation. The mind seems to possess an aspect that could be compared to a powerful spring, or to the string of a crossbow. When I am faced with some exciting challenge, I create mental energy by compressing the spring — or, to use the other image, by pulling back the string of the crossbow. In this battle to 'get on top' of experience, my most valuable weapon is knowledge, particularly self-knowledge. A child is far more vulnerable than an adult because the child's knowledge of the world is so much smaller, and he can easily be intimidated by tales of danger and disaster.

Consider a case recounted by Jung in the fourth chapter of *Psychology of the Unconscious*. A highly successful American businessman had worked his way up from the bottom, with the result that he was rich enough to retire at 45. But in spite of a marvellous estate and every possible form of amusement, he began to feel at a loose end. He became a hypochondriac and a nervous wreck. He consulted a psychiatrist, who recognized that the problem was lack of work, and recommended him to return to business. The man obeyed, but found to his dismay that business now bored him. When he consulted Jung, he was a 'hopeless moral ruin'. Jung felt he could do nothing for him. 'A case so far advanced can only be cared for until death; it can hardly be cured.'

Jung interpreted this case in terms of 'enantiodromia' —

a powerful emotion turning into its opposite, like St Paul's conversion on the road to Damascus. There were also traces, he said, of a mother fixation.

But Janet's theory provides a simpler and rather more satisfactory interpretation of the case. The businessman's psychological tension — and his sense of being 'on top of' his experience — was connected with his sense of purpose — of becoming successful. When he became successful and retired, his purpose vanished and his psychological tension collapsed. There was a lowering of the mental threshold. He was suddenly the victim rather than the master of his experience. Like a man lying awake in the middle of the night, he became subject to all kinds of absurd worries; and, never having had to keep himself amused — his career had always done it for him — he slipped into a vicious circle of self-pity and discouragement. Going back to work was no answer, for he had worked to be successful, and he *was* successful. Besides, with his lowered mental threshold, work would be disagreeable — like an invalid trying to plunge into cold water.

The theoretical solution of the problem would have been to utilize those characteristics of intelligence and ambition that had made him successful. If he could have been made to understand what had happened — as Janet could have made him understand — he would have realized that his salvation lay in breaking the vicious circle and seeking until he found one single subject or occupation that could arouse his interest. Above all, he would have to be made conscious that this was a problem that could be solved — like a bad cold or a headache — for raising the mental threshold depends on striking a spark of optimism, a conviction that something can be done. Jung's explanations about enantiodromia must have left him confused, bewildered and depressed — as Freud's explanations about his mother fixation and Oedipus complex would also have done. By approaching the problem with an unnecessarily complicated explanation — one that was, so to speak, too clever by a half — Jung had lost all chance of curing the patient.

The same unnecessarily complicated approach can be seen in another of Jung's cases. A teenage girl of good family had fallen into a state of schizophrenia, refusing even to speak. When Jung finally coaxed her into speaking, he discovered that she lived constantly in a fantasy that she was on the moon. It was her task to protect the moon people from a vampire covered in feathers; but when she tried to attack the vampire, he threw off the feathers and revealed himself as a handsome man with whom she fell in love . . .

Jung discovered that the girl had been seduced by her brother at the age of fifteen, and had later been sexually assaulted by a schoolmate — presumably a lesbian. His own explanation was that incest has always been a royal prerogative, and the girl's collective unconscious knew this. So she retreated to the moon — 'the mythic realm' — and became alienated from the real world.

Jung tells us that he eventually convinced her that she had to leave the moon and return to earth. At her first attempt to abandon her fantasy world she had a relapse; but she became 'resigned to her fate', and eventually married and had children.

Here again, Janet's explanation would be simple. The incest (which she presumably permitted) filled her with a sense of guilt that made her blush whenever she had to look her parents or teachers in the eyes. The sexual assault by the schoolmate increased her sense that sex is frightening and disgusting, something to be regretted. An adolescent has enough problems of adjustment to physical changes without being burdened with fear and guilt. The girl was clearly of an introverted and imaginative disposition — the kind who prefers reading or fantasizing to becoming involved in the real world. There was a lowering of the mental threshold, a vicious circle effect of fear and mistrust, and a loss of psychological tension. Her 'reality function' (another Janet concept) became enfeebled until she had no desire for contact with the real world, and retreated into a vivid fantasy. The story of the beautiful vampire reveals that her attitude to sex was by no means wholly negative; it strongly attracted as well as frightened her.

Here the cure was satisfactory because she happened to be female, and Jung could utilize the phenomenon of transference: a handsome young doctor trying to persuade her to return to earth. But the theories about incest and royalty and the mythic realm were totally irrelevant; they did not help Jung to solve the case, and add nothing to our understanding of it. They excite a definite feeling of 'sales resistance' in the reader — that Jung was determined to drag in his mythic theories whether they fitted or not. This could explain why a surprising number of Jung's cases — like the businessman, and Sir Montague Norman — ended in failure.

In fact, if psychology means understanding the *mechanisms* of the mind — what Gurdjieff meant by 'understanding the machine' — then Jung was not a particularly good psychologist. With his eyes fixed on his sonar gauges, looking for signs of what is going on in the black depths, he overlooks more straightforward mechanisms of neurosis. 'Enantiodromia', for example, seems to be an attempt to characterize what the Viennese psychiatrist Viktor Frankl later identified as 'the law of reverse effort' — the fact that when we are anxious to do something well, we do it badly. (Frankl's original insight came when he heard about a school play in which a boy who stuttered badly was chosen to play the part of a stutterer — and found that he spoke quite normally on stage.) But instead of recognizing its universal application, Jung has turned it into some deep psychic resistance that drives us to do the opposite of what we consciously desire: an altogether rarer phenomenon. The law of reverse effort affects all of us a dozen times a day because — as Thomson Jay Hudson recognized — we contain two people, and we are at our best when each one plays his own role, and does not interfere with the other. Consider a simple conundrum like: 'Brothers and sisters have I none, but this man's father is my father's son.' Some people find it impossible to work it out because the two people inside them get in one another's way and interfere with one another's efforts. As I write this page, one of the two persons inside me provides the 'insights', the other turns them into words, like a bricklayer and his assistant. If I am too anxious about the result, I strangle the insight. If I am too relaxed and confident, I may devote far too many words to some particular point. The two must try to fall into a comfortable rhythm that suits them both.

But their degree of cooperation depends on another factor. All creatures are partly mechanical; certain functions have been taken over by a kind of robot or automatic pilot. This robot not only drives my car; he arranges the words in my sentences. As a servant, he is indispensable. But if I go for a walk with my dogs, he becomes an unwelcome guest, for I would like to relax and enjoy the scenery, and my robot is still 'driving' me as he drives my car. The more complex my life is, the more efficient my robot needs to become, and the more difficult it is to persuade him to go off duty and allow me to appreciate things simply and directly. Modern man's reliance on alcohol, tobacco and drugs is an attempt to counteract the robot.

When we relax, we experience a sense of reality; we actually hear the birds and notice the trees. What the robot undermines is our *reality function*. So a modern city is full of people who have paid for their efficiency — their ability to survive — with an enfeebled sense of reality. Jung experienced this very clearly when he went to Africa and India, and his own robot realized it could relax its vigilance. But Jung's eyes were too fixed on the mythological archetypes to observe such a simple and obvious explanation for his sense of freedom and intensified reality.

In this situation, modern man finds it easy to slip into neurosis. Mental health depends upon the sense of reality, a constant 'feedback' between the mind and the environment. In this sense, we are like those small bivalves who live by sucking in water and shooting it out again. But, unlike the motion of the heart, this is *not* an automatic function. As soon as we grow tired or bored, we switch off the pump — and then wonder why we begin to experience a sense of suffocation. Modern man is continually slipping into this state of non-interaction, which results in a drop in vital energy. This in turn makes him feel that 'nothing is worth the effort', so he leaves the pump switched off. It is, in effect, as if he had forgotten to breathe. Then if problems arise that seem insoluble, he may experience a collapse of the will to live. Neurosis is a damaged will to live. Psychosis is the mind's attempt to compensate for the damaged will to live by providing an 'alternative reality'.

Now we can begin to see that both Freud and Jung had grasped this fundamental insight: that man has 'two selves', and that it is failure of cooperation between the two that causes mental illness. Freud's insight, like Hudson's, sprang from the observation of hypnosis, and the recognition that, when the ego is put to sleep, a non-ego can take over. Hudson called this non-ego 'the subjective mind', and recognized that its powers are far greater than those of the 'objective mind'. Freud called it the unconscious; but he failed to grasp — what Hudson understood so well — that in the last analysis, the objective mind is the 'boss'. *It* is the part of us that recognizes values, that generates a sense of purpose, that sees what has to be done, and which sends a message down to the subjective mind demanding energy. (The subjective mind is in charge of our energy supply — what the playwright Granville Barker called 'the secret life'.) It is *its* vigilance, its enthusiasm and determination, that govern our mental health. Whenever we are hurled into purposeful activity, we recognize this clearly. (This is why the philosopher Fichte remarked that man only knows himself in action.) Unfortunately, man spends so much of his time in passivity, or in repetitious acts, that he finds it easy to forget this insight.

Because Freud took it for granted that the objective mind has no power at all, his psychology was essentially negative and pessimistic in character. Neurosis was due to unconscious sexual repression, and the only way to cure the neurosis was for the analyst to uncover the repression and drag it into the light of consciousness. The patient was not in any way encouraged to take a positive attitude towards his problems. The result was that many of Freud's cases dragged on for years, and ended without a cure (for example, the famous 'Wolf man').

Jung felt instinctively that Freud's negative and passive view of the unconscious was wrong. He cured his 'vampire' lady by telling her that she had to come down to earth and stop longing for the moon. He also recognized that Janet had grasped the basic cause of neurosis in his 'lowering of the mental threshold'. But for an ambitious young psychiatrist, the embattled Freud was a far more interesting figure to support than the well-established, middle-aged Janet. So Jung found himself committed to Freud's view of the 'second self' as an unfathomable ocean or some vast underground kingdom. This was certainly a more exciting view than Janet's; besides, Jung saw himself inheriting Freud's position and becoming the lord of this romantic and sinister underworld.

The quarrel with Freud and Jung's own sense of guilt produced tremendous psychological tensions. When psychological tensions persist for too long, the result is exhaustion, and the normal distinction between dreams and waking consciousness disappears. Jung experienced the mythological visions — Siegfried, Salome, Philemon — that convinced him that his own interpretation of the unconscious was correct after all. It also meant that he created a psychological theory of 'projections' to explain religion, alchemy, flying saucers and anything else that puzzled him. In fact, it failed to explain the first case he ever encountered — his cousin Helly's multiple personality. But he dismissed the problem by assuming she was merely a fantasist and a liar. Later, when he encountered genuine mediumship (in Rudi Schneider) and recognized that ghosts are not necessarily 'projections', he took care not to revise his views on Helly Preiswerk.

If, in fact, we recognize Jung's 'confrontation with the unconscious' as a highly abnormal state, in which his 'second self' came to his aid with the reassurance he needed, his theory of projections appears rather more questionable. There is no conceivable reason to believe that hundreds of alchemists, from ancient Greece and China to medieval Europe, all experienced visions that explain their strange images and terminology. It is far more probable that the alchemists were working within a magical tradition (and magic and science were identical in the past) and using its language and images. Jung's essays on Paracedsus show that he was aware that he was dealing vith an alien intellectual tradition; but his determination to use it to prove his theory of archetypes and projections made him incapable of entering into its spirit.

The case of the flying saucers offers a more straightforward example of the problem. The possibility that most UFO sightings are 'visions' is obviously remote. Some may be downright lies, some wishful thinking, some honest mistakes; but there remain a number — when a whole planeload of passengers have seen the craft — where none of these explanations will fit. Jung's 'projection' theory is far less likely than the notion that the witness saw *something* — whether an experimental aircraft, a messenger from another planet, or a visitor from another dimension. But the projectiOn theory happened to fit in with his theory of archetypes and unconscious religious cravings. So the facts could be ignored. His book on UFOs is virtually propaganda for his archetype theory, designed to reach a new and vast audience. From the interview with Lindbergh(it is clear that either Jung himself did not believe his own theory, or that he had changed his mind since he wrote the book. In any case, he kept his views a secret. Lindbergh seems to have sensed this when he remarked on the element of charlatanism in Jung.

I have pointed out in the Introduction that Jung's views on the paranormal also contain this element of 'double-think'. The essay on 'The Psychological Foundations of Belief in Spirits' interprets them as 'autonomous complexes'. His own experience of the haunted cottage, as well as his seances with Rudi Schneider, must have made him aware that this was simply inadequate as an explanation. (Anyone who wishes to gain an idea of what happened with Schneider should read Thomas Mann's essay 'An Experience with the Occult'.* (In a cautious postscript to this essay written in 1948, he tried to qualify his arguments. He had 'confined himself wholly to the psychological side of the problem, and purposely avoided the question of whether spirits exist'. He goes on to tell a lie: that he has had no experience that might prove it one way or the other. The preface to Fanny Moser's book on ghosts reveals that he accepted his experience in the cottage as a genuine haunting: when he learned that the owner had been forced to demolish the cottage 'it gave me considerable satisfaction after my colleague had laughed so loudly at my fear of ghosts'. But this introduction was not printed beside the essay 'On the Psychological Foundations of Belief in Spirits' in Volume Eight of the Collected Works — where the contradiction would be obvious — but in the 'miscellaneous' Volume Eighteen.

The important question is obviously: How far do these inconsistencies undermine Jung's total achievement? And this can only be answered in the broader perspective of what he was trying to do — and not, it must be

* Discussed in my book *The Occult* (1971), pp. 219-20.

emphasized, what he wanted his colleagues to believe he was trying to do.

Jung had the temperament to be an artist, a poet or a theologian. If his father had been rich he might, like the Mann brothers, have spent a year or so in Italy, deciding what he wanted to do. As it was he was forced to choose medicine — far too rigid a discipline for a person of Jung's originality and ambition. Like the young Americans addressed by Horace Greely, ('Go West, young man'), his real desire was to find virgin territory and adventure; but Europe had no Wild West, and Jung chose psychiatry instead.

There is some significance in Jung's belief — or his occasional claim — that he was a descendant of Goethe. He was completely out of sympathy with the narrow materialism of nineteenth-century science. In retrospect, it seems a pity he became a Freudian, since it meant he based his life work on Freud's premises about the unconscious. Yet it has to be admitted that, as a follower of Janet, he might not have achieved such remarkable results. In an essay on Wagner, Thomas Mann quoted a dignitary of Seville cathedral, who is supposed to have said to the architect: 'Build me a cathedral so enormous that people of the future will say: the chapter must have been mad to build anything so huge . . . ' Mann pointed out that the nineteenth century was full of this spirit of heroic giganticism: Balzac's *Human Comedy*, Hegel's System, Zola's Rougon Macquart cycle, Wagner's *Ring*, Tolstoy's *War and Peace*. Jung's sympathy was all with heroic giganticism. His psychology is built of the same mythological material as Wagner's *Ring*.

His central insight was the same as Hudson's: that the immense powers of the 'subjective mind' can be utilized for positive as well as negative purposes. Although he insisted that his interest in religion was purely 'psychological' (an assertion that seems absurd in the light of *Answer to Job*), the basic assumption of his work was identical with that of all the major religions: that the universe is full of meaning, that we are surrounded by unseen powers and forces, and that man can rise above the 'triviality of everydayness' by trying to open his mind and his senses to these meanings and forces.

Freud's negative vision of the unconscious invalidates

much of his work; it seems conceivable that, in the future, his psychology will be regarded merely as an intellectual curiosity, like the phlogiston theory of combustion, or Hoerbiger's belief that the moon is a huge lump of ice. Most psychologists would now agree that the sexual theory cannot be regarded as 'scientifically proven'. Jung's archetypes and collective unconscious are in the same dubious position. But Jung's vision of the unconscious is of an enormous wellspring of vital forces. The author of a recent book about him* has pointed out the similarities between Jung and Abraham Maslow, whose psychology is based on the notion of 'higher reaches of human nature', and who was more interested in the 'peak experience' — the sense of sudden affirmation — than in neurosis. There can be no doubt that Jung's *weltanschauung* is pervaded by an enormous sense of optimism, of the possibilities of human evolution.

His central concept is, of course, individuation, meaning 'undividedness'. In *Answer to Job* he has the important comment: 'the more consciousness a man possesses the more he is separated from his instincts (which at least give him an inkling of the hidden wisdom of God) and the more prone he is to error.' Man's problem is that, in the course of evolving consciousness, he has become divided from his unconscious, which contains inklings of the purposes and aims of God. The answer is for consciousness to attempt to achieve contact with the unconscious — in fact, ideally, to have free access to it. Jung discovered at an early stage that the practice of meditation is one way of achieving contact, and the experience of Africa showed him that man can 'relax into' his unconscious by recognizing the 'dark' side of his nature.

Yet although Jung was attempting to create a dynamic and positive vision of the psyche to replace Freud's passive and negative model, his Freudian training made it difficult for him to emphasize the notion of conscious effort. Towards the end of his life, he was asked by E. H. Philp: 'Is it possible that you depreciate consciousness through an overvaluation of the unconscious?', and replied decisively: 'I have never had any tendency to

* John-Raphael Staude: *The Adult Development of C.G. Jung* (1981).

depreciate consciousness by insisting upon the importance of the unconscious. If such a tendency is attributed to
me, it is due to a sort of optical illusion.' Readers of
Symbols of Transformation, or even of *Aion*, must have
shaken their heads in startled disbelief. But at least Jung
goes on to reveal how far he has come to recognize the
importance of consciousness — and therefore, by implication, of its power of making decisions. 'As a matter of fact
the emphasis lies on consciousness as the *conditio sine qua
non* of apperception of unconscious contents, and the
supreme arbiter [my italics] in the chaos of unconscious
possibilities. My book about *Types* is a careful study of the
empirical structure of consciousness. If we had an inferior
consciousness, we should all be crazy. The ego and
ego-consciousness are of paramount importance.'

But more than a quarter of a century earlier, in his
Commentary on *The Secret of the Golden Flower*, Jung had
written: 'Now and then it happend in my practice that a
patient grew beyond himself because of unknown potentialities . . . What did these people do in order to bring
about the development that set them free? As far as I could
see they did nothing (*wu wei*) but let things happen.'
Again, in the second of the *Two Essays on Analytical
Psychology* (Volume Seven of the Collected Works) there is
a chapter dealing with individuation in which Jung
identifies it with self-realization. But it is clear that he sees
self-realization as springing from the unconscious. He
speaks, for example, of lazy people who have ended as
neurotics, and says: 'Thanks to the neurosis contrived by
the unconscious, they are shaken out of their apathy . . .'
A paragraph further on he writes: 'Since it is highly
probable that we are still a long way from the summit of
absolute consciousness, presumably everyone is capable
of wider consciousness, and we may assume accordingly
that the unconscious processes are constantly supplying
us with contents which, if consciously recognized, would
extend the range of consciousness.'

This makes it quite clear that for Jung, the work of
individuation — self-realization — consists basically in
'listening to' the unconscious, which is trying to push us
towards self-realization. So in place of Freud's negative
unconscious, which causes so many neuroses, we have a
positive unconscious trying to work out our salvation. It is

an agreeable notion; but Hudson could have told Jung that he was overestimating the subjective mind. The subjective mind may be far more powerful than its objective counterpart, but in this particular marriage, it is the passive partner. It will place its enormous powers and energies at the disposal of the objective mind — if the objective mind demands them with enough authority — but will seldom take the initiative. Hypnosis is so successful because the subjective mind is glad to obey the authoritative voice of the hypnotist. It would obey the objective mind just as readily, if the order was delivered with enough conviction. But most people are possessed by the misapprehension that the ego is supposed to be passive, that their business is to suffer and accept experience rather than initiate it. We might compare the two to a husband and wife team in which the wife has tremendous untapped energies and potentialities. But she is married to a feeble and passive husband. And she has been brought up to believe that the woman is supposed to be docile and obedient. So because the husband never calls upon her untapped resources, she fails to achieve any kind of self-realization. The answer is not for the wife to leave the husband or try to 'do her own thing', but for the husband to recognize that if he can galvanize himself out of his feebleness and laziness, they can transform both their lives.

Let us look more closely at this concept of individuation. Why does Jung regard it as a passive process? Because he sees it as a flow from the unconscious to the conscious. It *has* to be that way around because the conscious, has, so to speak, no way of clambering down a ladder into the unconscious. And this seems to be one of the fundamental problems. Jung's answer to it consists in creating the right conditions (as Africa and India created them for him), or (in the case of patients) in trying to tease the problems out of the unconscious by the usual methods of psychoanalysis. The therapist is, so to speak, the midwife to the unconscious.

We can clarify the issue if, instead of speaking of the conscious and unconscious, we revert to Hudson' terminology of the objective and subjective mind — or of the left and right cerebral hemispheres, which seem to bear such a close relation to them. When Sperry was doing his early experiments in split-brain physiology, he discovered that an animal with a split brain cannot pass on something it has just learned to the other half of the brain — so a split-brain cat that had been taught to press a lever to get food with one eye covered up could not do the same trick with the other eye covered. The purpose of the commissure between the two halves is to pass on such information to the other half of the brain. So there *is* a mechanism for communication — for what Jung called the individuation process.

But it is such an inefficient mechanism that, for all practical purposes, we are all split-brain patients. In *Biographia Literaria*, Coleridge cites a remarkable case of an ignorant servant girl who began speaking Hebrew when she was in delirium. Eventually it was discovered that, as a small girl, she had lived in the house of a clergyman who went around reciting the Bible in Hebrew. Consciously she had never picked up a word of the language; but her subjective mind had stored up everything she had overheard.

So the subjective mind contains *everything* we have ever seen, heard and experienced. And it will, under certain circumstances, provide us with the information we require. I try to remember a name or a tune without success. I stop trying, and suddenly it 'walks into my head' — that is, into my objective mind, sent there by the subjective mind. I tell myself I must wake at half past six in the morning, but I have no alarm clock; my subjective mind shakes me awake at precisely six-thirty.

Moreover, when my objective mind is sent to sleep by a hypnotist, my subjective mind will provide all kinds of information on request. It merely needs to be asked properly.

It has another interesting trick. A tune or a smell or a few words can suddenly bring back some fragment of my past with tremendous vividness, so for a moment I am back in the 'den' made of branches I constructed when I was eight, or the school changing room when I was twelve. Proust based his enormous novel on such 'flashes' — glimpses of the past. In my book *The Occult* I used the term 'Faculty X' for this ability to conjure up the *reality* of some other time and place. What Jung means by individuation is closely related to Faculty X.

Is it — to rephrase the question — possible to *induce* flashes of Faculty X, or do we have to wait patiently until they burst upon us? Maslow raised a similar question when he asked whether it is possible to induce the 'peak experience'; he decided that the answer was No: we have to wait for it to happen.

But consider more closely the mechanism of such experiences. In *The Idiot*, Dostoevsky describes the feelings of a man in front of a firing squad. He is fascinated by a gilded steeple glittering in the sunlight, and feels that in a few moments he will be one with the rays of light. He wonders what would happen if he were reprieved (as, in fact, he is), and thinks 'What an eternity of days, and all mine! How I should grudge and count up every minute of it, so as not to waste a single instant.' The murderer Raskolnikov has a similar insight in *Crime and Punishment*, when he reflects that he would rather stand on a narrow ledge for ever, in eternal darkness and tempest, than be condemned to die at once.

Crisis makes human beings suddenly aware of what consciousness is *for*. Its purpose is to *control* our lives. About to be deprived of it, the prisoner feels that if only he could be reprieved, he would never again waste a single instant.

This enables us to grasp precisely what is wrong with man at this stage in his evolution. We *waste* consciousness by drifting passively through life. Civilization has separated us from our deep, instinctive will to live, eroded our 'reality function'. As Jung recognized, man has developed too fast, and consciousness has drifted too far from the deep knowledge of the unconscious. So, like an army whose baggage train has fallen too far behind, we are highly vulnerable.

The problem, quite simply, is that consciousness is still too feeble. Crises and problems galvanize us into a sense of values, and make us recognize how hard we *ought* to be struggling. But the moment the crisis is behind us, we *forget* this insight, and drift back into a vague state of non-expectation, 'living in the present' and allowing all our vital energy, our psychological tension, to drain away. Molehills turn into mountains. This is why modern man is so prone to neurosis. His ego becomes 'hypnotized' by the trivialities of the present and his vital 'threshold' sinks. In this state he becomes convinced that he is weak and helpless — although, in fact, he possesses enormous strength, which would respond to the first sign of crisis.

William James had recognized the problem when he wrote that what modern man needs to find is the 'moral equivalent of war'. And in an essay 'The Energies of Man' he stated the problem with unparalleled clarity:

> Compared to what we ought to be, we are only half awake. Our fires are damped, our drafts are checked. We are making use of only a small part of our possible mental and physical resources. In some persons this sense of being cut off from their rightful resources is extreme, and we then get the formidable neurasthenic and psychasthenic conditions, with life grown into one tissue of impossibilities, that so many medical books describe.
>
> Stating the thing broadly, the human individual thus lives usually far within his limits; he possesses powers of various sorts which he habitually fails to use. He energises below his maximum, and he behaves below his optimum.

How can man escape this trap, and release his 'vital reserves'? James's answer is that 'the normal opener of deeper and deeper levels of energy is the will'. 'Excitements, ideas and efforts, in a word, are what carry us over the dam.' Yet James had to admit that he could not actually suggest a 'moral equivalent of war' that would galvanize all men to energize to their maximum.

We could say that Jung picked up the problem where James left off. He also began from the recognition that man contains immense depths of power of which he is normally unaware. And his own solution to the problem was to spend his life directing attention to these depths. He turned his back on his Freudian training, and presented a new and vital image of the psyche. His aim, we could say, was to direct man's attention inward. The philosopher David Hume protested that when he turned his gaze inward, he only perceived ideas and emotions, a 'stream of consciousness' flowing endlessly and automatically. Jung's reply, in effect, is: 'Look deeper still'. Strain the eyes into that realm of dreams and symbols until they become used to the darkness. Gradually, the conscious ego will become aware that it has a far more powerful partner, that it is not alone. Man will begin to catch glimpses of his own strength. The process of individuation will begin, like an alchemical transformation. What will eventually emerge is the philosopher's stone.

Let us raise the question that Jung leaves unexplored: what would it be like to experience individuation? What would it be like if the conscious mind had unlimited access to the unconscious — if the objective mind could explore the subjective mind at will?

It would mean, to begin with, that the enormous powers of the subjective mind would become accessible to the ego. It contains, for example, all the memories of a lifetime. Because consciousness is so narrow, we are trapped in a tiny prison cell of the present. So our view of ourselves is also narrow and limited. When Proust's hero tasted the cake dipped in tea, he said: 'I had ceased to feel mediocre, accidental, mortal.' Faust, on the point of suicide, is recalled to life by the Easter bells, and remembers how, in childhood,

> An unbelievably sweet yearning
> Drove me to roam through wood and lea,
> Crying, and as my eyes were burning,
> I felt a new world grow in me.

What we glimpse in such moments is that if consciousness could move beyond its normal limitations, we could easily experience a kind of chain reaction into mystical ecstasy. The delight, the sense of meaning, of other realities, other times and places, releases an immense surge of optimism and purpose. This in turn is enough to raise us permanently to a higher level of vital drive and determination — for, like a man who has glimpsed heaven, nothing less can now ever satisfy us.

Then there are the other powers of the subjective mind: its apparently paranormal powers, its powers to heal and renew the body, its ability to induce synchronicities, its fathomless creative powers. All these, it seems, are there for the asking, if only we could start the chain reaction by some immense effort of will and optimism — or, as Jung suggests, by inducing the unconscious to make the effort.

This is the essence of Jung's vision, his glimpse of the philosopher's stone. It is, of course, necessary to recognize that Jung himself failed to achieved the philosopher's stone, and that this was probably because his life was a little too comfortable, and because he became a little too accustomed to getting his own way. We might say that the crucible never became hot enough. This is no denigration of his formidable achievement: only a recognition of an element on which he failed to place sufficient emphasis: conscious effort.

But then, we judge a man of genius by his central insight. Jung's central insight was a development of the vision of his youth, and it was a message of hope for his fellow men. He achieved what he set out to achieve — an epitaph good enough for any man.

Appendix

Active Imagination

Active imagination is certainly one of the most interesting and exciting of all Jung's ideas. But those who wish to learn more about it will have a frustrating time searching through the Collected Works; the General Index lists a few dozen references, but most of these turn out to be merely passing mentions. The earliest — and perhaps most complete — description of the method occurs in the essay on 'The Transcendent Function', written in 1916; yet here Jung does not even mention it by name. Moreover, he left the essay in his files until someone asked him for a contribution to a student magazine in 1957. It appears in Volume Eight of the Collected Works, together with a preliminary warning: 'The method is . . . not without its dangers, and should, if possible, not be employed except under expert supervision.'

Yet if the method is as effective as Jung claims — in his autobiography — then such a danger should not be taken too seriously. After all, *if* active imagination really works, then Jung has solved a problem that tormented so many of the 'outsiders' of the nineteenth century, and should have provided mankind with a vital key to its future evolution. In a letter of 1871 Rimbaud wrote about the poet's need to induce visions: 'I say that one must be a *visionary* — that one must make oneself a VISIONARY.' He goes on: 'The poet makes himself a *visionary* through a long, immense and reasoned *derangement of all the senses*. All forms of love, of suffering, of madness, he seeks himself . . . ' And in *A Season in Hell*, he claims to have succeeded in inducing this derangement: 'I accustomed myself to simple hallucination: I really saw a mosque in place of a factory, angels practising on drums, coaches on the roads of the sky; a drawing room at the bottom of a lake: monsters, mysteries . . . '

But when expressed in this form, we can see that it is basically the old romantic craving for wonders, marvels and ecstasies, the craving expressed in the very title of Poe's *Tales of Mystery and Imagination*. We find it in the dim, misty landscapes of Novalis and Tieck, in the grotesqueries of Hoffmann and Jean Paul, in the horrors of Poe and Sheridan Le Fanu, in the courtly daydreams of the Pre-Raphaelites, in Aubrey Beardsley's erotic imagery (and it was Beardsley who outraged readers of the *Yellow Book* with the image of a grand piano in a field) and in the shock tactics of the surrealists and the Dadaists. It all seems to amount to Yeat's attempt to escape the 'foul rag and bone shop of the heart' with a kind of ladder of wishful thinking. Clearly, if Jung had really created a usable technique for 'making oneself a visionary' and seeing angels practising on drums and drawing rooms at the bottom of a lake, then this alone would qualify him as one of the most significant figures of our century.

It was in the autobiography that Jung made clear for the first time how he came to recognize the existence of active imagination: how the break with Freud brought him to the verge of total nervous collapse, and so allowed him a glimpse of the delusions suffered by psychotic patients. It was fortunate for Jung that the vision of Europe drowned in blood came true in the following year, bringing the recognition that an 'illusion' is not necessarily untrue. 'I see too deep and too much' says the 'Outsider' hero of Barbusse's *L'Enfer*, and this was precisely what was happening to Jung.

When the mind is under this kind of severe stress, its natural tendency is to put up frantic resistance. Jung recognized that he was in the same position as Nietzsche and Hölderlin, and that, like them, he might lose his sanity; the result was a grim determination not to 'let go'. Then, in December 1913, sitting at his desk in a state of turmoil and pessimism, he made the momentous decision to 'let go' and see what happened. The result was not total breakdown: it was the astonished recognition that the force that had been trying to make him let go was a stranger inside his own head, and that the stranger was in perfect control of the situation. It was a blinding recognition of the 'hidden ally'. In Hudson's terms, what was happening was that the 'subjective mind' was saying to the 'objective mind': 'Look, for heaven's sake stop struggling to maintain this iron curtain between us, because you're wasting your strength in fighting yourself.' It could be compared to a wife saying to her husband, who is exhausted by driving: 'Get in the back and have a nap while I drive.' Jung was sensible enough to let go of the steering wheel, and the result was the 'waking dream' of the cave with the corpse of Siegfried.

In a book called *Access to Inner Worlds* I have described how a similar experience happened to an American living in Finland, Brad Absetz. After the death of their child through cancer, his wife collapsed into severe depression. She used to lie on a bed for hours, plunged in negative fantasies and self-reproaches; Brad Absetz lay beside her, waiting for her to emerge, so he could be there to help her. He lay in a state of vigilance, waiting for the slightest indication that she was 'coming round'; at the same time, he was physically relaxed. One day, as he lay there, he experienced an overwhelming sense of lightness and relief, almost as if he were floating up off the bed. This was his own equivalent of Jung's 'letting go'. And what now happened was that that 'other person' inside his head began to express itself. As he stood by the buffet table, waiting to help himself to lunch, his arm began to twitch; he recognized this as a signal that it wanted to do something, and allowed it to reach out and take whatever food it liked. It took food that he would not normally have taken. This continued for weeks, and in a short time, he had lost weight, and felt healthier than ever before. One day his small daughter asked him to make her a drawing with coloured crayons; again, the hand began to twitch, and he allowed it to do what it liked. The result was an astonishing series of drawings and paintings, incredible 'psychedelic' patterns, every one totally different from all the others. His 'other self' took over and wrote poetry, while he merely looked on; it made metal sculptures; it performed his everyday tasks — like bee-keeping — in a simple, ritualistic manner that renewed his vitality. In the parliament of Brad's mind, the Member for the Unconscious had been given his proper say, and the result was a life that was in every way more harmonious and relaxed. He had, to a large extent, achieved 'individuation'.

Brad Absetz was in no danger of insanity when he 'let

go', but he was under severe stress. His subjective mind, left to its own devices, showed him the way out of the impasse. (The method — of lying totally relaxed, but in a state of wide-awake vigilance — could be regarded as the simplest and most effective of all mental therapies.)

In 1913, Jung was in a rather worse state; so when he 'let go', the image-making powers of the subjective mind flooded into consciousness. He called the result 'active imagination', but we can see that it was not imagination in the ordinary sense of the word: the deliberate evocation of mental images or states. What Jung had achieved was a *new balance* between the ego and the unconscious, in which the unconscious was recognized as an equal partner. This explains why, from then on, Jung frequently had 'visions', like the one of the crucified Christ at the end of his bed.

We can at once see the difference between Jung's concept of active imagination and Rimbaud's. Rimbaud *talked* about surrendering to suffering and madness; but in effect, his ego remained in charge. He attempted a 'reasoned derangement of the senses' with drugs and alcohol, but since his ego was strong, these failed to produce individuation and 'access to inner worlds.' (I am inclined to regard his statement that he accustomed himself to seeing mosques instead of factories, etc, as wishful thinking, poetic license.) The real 'breakthrough' tends to occur in moments of desperation, or under extreme stress, and is a kind of inspired surrender. (Ramakrishna achieved a similar breakthrough when he attempted suicide with a sword, and was suddenly overwhelmed by a vision of the Divine Mother.)

Now we can begin to see why, although Jung regarded active imagination as the key to 'individuation', he said very little about it. There was very little to say. In the essay on 'The Transcendent Function' he writes: *'In the intensity of the emotional disturbance itself lies the value, the energy which he should have at his disposal in order to remedy the state . . .'* He adds: 'Nothing is achieved by repressing this state or devaluing it rationally.' In other words, the patient suffering from severe mental stress is already ideally placed to begin to develop active imagination.

Jung's instructions follow:

In order, therefore, to gain possession of the energy that is in the wrong place, he must make the emotional state the basis or starting point of the procedure. He must make himself as conscious as possible of the mood he is in, sinking himself in it without reserve and noting down on paper all the fantasies and other associations that come up. Fantasy must be allowed the freest possible play, yet not in such a manner that it leaves the orbit of its object . . . by setting off a kind of 'chain-reaction' process. This 'free association', as Freud called it, leads away from the object to all sorts of complexes . . .

He utters a similar warning in the introduction he wrote to the essay in 1958: that 'one of the lesser dangers [of the method] is that [it] may not lead to any positive result, since it easily passes over into the so-called "free association" of Freud, whereupon the patient gets caught in the sterile circle of his own complexes . . .' We can see that, for example, if Brad Absetz had lain on the bed 'free associating', he would never have achieved the breakthrough; what was so important was the combination of total relaxation with mental *vigilance* and alertness. 'The whole procedure', says Jung, 'is a kind of enrichment and clarification of the affect [powerful feeling-state], whereby the affect and its contents are brought nearer to consciousness.' In some cases, says Jung, the patient may actually *hear* the 'other voice' as an auditory hallucination — a comment that will convince split-brain psychologists that Jung is talking about the right and left cerebral hemispheres.

All this may leave readers who were hoping to learn how to practise active imagination feeling a little frustrated. Let us see if the matter can be clarified.

The essence of Jung's original experience — of 'waking dreams' — was the *recognition* of the reality of the 'hidden ally'. The 'letting go' that revealed this ally was a rather frightening process — like letting yourself fall backwards, hoping someone is standing there to catch you (a game many of us used to play as children). Once you have discovered that there *is* someone waiting to catch you, the fear vanishes and turns into a sense of confidence and reassurance.

We could say, then, that the correct starting point for active imagination is the recognition that there *is* someone standing there behind you. In a remarkable book called *The Secret Science at Work*, Max Freedom Long describes his own methods — based upon those of the Hunas of Hawaii — for contacting the 'hidden ally' (which he calls the 'low self'); Long's group began referring to the 'other self' as George, and found that it could be engaged in a dialogue (and could also answer questions by means of a pendulum).

Once the *real existence* of the 'other self' has been recognized, the next question is to tease it into expressing itself. In a letter of 1947, Jung explained his technique to a Mrs O-:

> The point is that you start with any image, for instance just with that yellow mass in your dream. Contemplate it and carefully observe how the picture begins to unfold or change. Don't try to make it into something, just do nothing but observe what its spontaneous changes are. Any mental picture you contemplate in this way will sooner or later change through a spontaneous association that causes a slight alteration of the picture . . . Hold fast to the one image you have chosen and wait until it changes by itself. Note all these changes and eventually step into the picture yourself, and if it is a speaking figure . . . then say what you have to say to that figure and listen to what he or she has to say.

In his Tavistock Lectures of 1935 (Collected Works, Vol. 18) Jung gives an example of how one of his patients finally achieved active imagination 'from cold', so to speak. He was a young artist who seemed to find it practically impossible to understand what Jung meant by active imagination. 'This man's brain was always working for itself'; that is to say, his artistic ego would not get out of the driving seat. But each time the artist came to see Jung, he waited at a small station, and looked at a poster advertising Mürren, in the Bernese Alps; it had a waterfall, a green meadow and a hill with cows. He decided to try 'fantasizing' about the poster. He stared at it and imagined he was in the meadow, then that he was walking up the hill. Perhaps he was in a particularly relaxed mood that day, or perhaps his artistic imagination now came to his aid instead of obstructing him. (We can imagine his right brain saying: 'So *that's* what you wanted! Why didn't you say so?') A waking dream took over. He found himself walking along a footpath on the other side of the hill, round a ravine and a large rock, and into a little chapel. As he looked at the face of the Virgin on the altar, something with pointed ears vanished behind the altar. He thought 'That's all nonsense', and the fantasy was gone.

He was struck by the important thought: perhaps that was not fantasy — perhaps it was really there. Now presumably on the train, he closed his eyes and conjured up the scene again. Again he entered the chapel, and again the thing with pointed ears jumped behind the altar. This was enough to convince him that what he had seen was not mere fantasy, but a genuine glimpse of an *objective reality* inside his own head, 'access to inner worlds'. This, says Jung, was the beginning of a successful development of active imagination.

What becomes very clear here is that there is a certain 'turning point', and that this is the moment when the subject suddenly realizes that this is not mere personal fantasy, but that he is dealing with an objective reality — the reality we occasionally encounter in dreams, when some place seems totally real.

The basic procedure, then, seems to be: lie still — as Brad Absetz did — and become perfectly relaxed and yet fully alert. Place yourself in a *listening* frame of mind, waiting for 'George' to speak. That is to say, assume that there *is* someone there who has something to communicate, and ask him to go ahead and say it. If what he 'says' is an image, then contemplate it as you might contemplate a painting in an art gallery, and ask him, so to speak, to go on.

Julian Jaynes's book *The Origin of Consciousness in the Breakdown of the Bicameral Mind* may be found a useful accessory in this quest for 'the turning point'. Jaynes believes that our remote ancestors of four thousand years ago did not possess 'self-consciousness' in the sense that we do; they could not decide a course of action by 'questioning themselves', because their minds were turned outward, so to speak. Decisions were made for them by 'voices' that came into their heads, and which they mistook for the voices of the gods; in fact, it was the other half of the brain, the 'other self'. Later, Jaynes believed, war and crisis forced man to develop self-awareness, so he no longer had need of auditory hallucinations.

We may object to this theory on the grounds that modern man is *still* 'bicameral' (with two minds), and that therefore it seems more probable that ancient man was 'unicameral', in a relaxed, 'instinctive' state of oneness with nature, like a cow. But this objection makes no real difference to the substance of the theory, which springs from the scientific recognition that we actually possess a 'second self' in the brain, and that thousands of people experience this second self in the form of auditory and visual hallucinations — what Jung called 'projections'.

In her book *Encounters with the Soul: Active Imagination*, the Jungian psychotherapist Barbara Hannah insists that ancient man's encounters with 'God' (in the Old Testament, for example) are instances of active imagination: that is, of the action of the 'bicameral mind'. She cites two highly convincing examples of the 'auditory method of active imagination' from 2200 BC and from AD 1200, then reprints an important modern document, the account of a patient called Anna Marjula, of how she was cured through the practice of active imagination. The case helps to throw light on what Jung meant by active imagination.

Anna Marjula was the daughter of a lawyer, and Jung thought the origin of her neurosis could have been sexual — seeing her father masturbating when she was a small girl; the father later revealed a certain physical interest in his daughter. She was a shy, nervous child, tormented by feelings of inferiority, and the death of her mother was a shattering experience. She was a fine musician, and wanted to become a concert pianist. Working for her examination, at the age of twenty-one, she became over-tense and spiritually exhausted. On the night before the examination, she had a 'vision'. A voice told her to sacrifice ambition, and to be perfectly willing to accept failure. (This, we can see, was the best advice her subjective mind could have offered her.) Her willingness to accept possible defeat brought religious ecstasy; at this point, the 'voice' told her that she was not destined to become famous herself, but that her real vocation was to become the mother of a man of genius. She should look around for someone who would be the right father for a man of genius, and offer herself to him without physical desire. If she could succeed in conceiving a child without any feeling of pleasure, the result would be a man of genius.

In fact, the patient never met the right man, and as she entered her forties, a conviction of having 'missed the boat' caused severe psychological problems. She was fifty-one when she became Jung's patient.

The analyst — Jung's wife — suggested that the original 'vision' was a deception of the 'animus', and that the patient should try to use active imagination to approach a more positive female archetype, the Great Mother. Clearly, the patient already had a predisposition to 'visions', and her psychological tensions provided the psychic energy for active imagination. The result was a remarkable series of conversations with the 'Great Mother', in which the patient experienced the Mother as another person — as Jung experienced Philemon. The eventual result, according to Barbara Hannah, was a happy and serene old age.

Another Jungian analyst, J. Marvin Spiegelman, set out to conquer the techniques of active imagination at the age of twenty-four, with 'fantasies' of a cave, in which he encountered a mother, daughter and a wise old man. One day, a knight appeared and carried off the mother and daughter. The knight explained that he had certain tales to tell, and that there were 'several others in his realm' who also wished to dictate their stories. Spiegelman then spent several years taking down various stories dictated by the knight, a nun, a nymphomaniac, an old Chinaman, and various others: these were published in four volumes. Clearly, Spiegelman had used the same technique as Brad Absetz — allowing the 'other self' to overcome its shyness and express itself — and the results were in many ways similar.

In the fourth volume of the series, *The Knight*, Spiegelman makes an observation of central importance: that the successful practice of active imagination 'regularly leads to the occurrence of synchronistic events, in which one is related to the world in a deep, mystical way'. What happens, Spiegelman suggests, is that the inner work somehow changes one's relationship to the world. He then tells the important story of the Rainmaker, originally told to Jung by Richard Wilhelm. Wilhelm was in a remote

Chinese village that was suffering from drought. A rainmaker was sent for from a distant village. He asked for a cottage on the outskirts of the village, and vanished into it for three days. Then there was a tremendous downpour, followed by snow — an unheard-of occurrence at that time of year.

Wilhelm asked the old man how he had done it; the old man replied that he hadn't. 'You see', said the old man, 'I come from a region where everything is in order. It rains when it should rain and is fine when that is needed. The people are themselves in order. But the people in this village are all out of Tao and out of themselves. I was at once infected when I arrived, so I asked for a cottage on the edge of the village, so I could be alone. When I was once more in Tao, it rained.'

By being 'in Tao and in themselves', the old man meant what Jung meant by individuation. That is to say, there was a proper traffic between the two selves — or the two halves of the brain. The people in the rainless village were dominated by the left-brain ego — which, while it is unaware of the 'hidden ally', is inclined to over-react to problems. This in turn produces a negative state of mind that can influence the external world.

This throws a wholly new light on the idea of synchronicity, and also of magic. One could say that, according to the Chinese theory, the mind is intimately involved with nature. Synchronicity is not therefore the active intervention of the mind in natural processes: rather, a natural product of their harmony. (So when we are psychologically healthy, synchronicities should occur all the time.) Our fears and tensions interfere with this natural harmony; when this happens, things go wrong.

We can see that this also changes our concept of the nature of active imagination. It is *not* some kind of 'reasoned derangement of the senses', directed by the ego. It is an inner harmony based on the recognition of the 'hidden ally', which leads to a process of cooperation between the 'two selves'.

But here again, a warning must be uttered. A remarkable American physician, Howard Miller, has pointed out that human beings already possess a form of active imagination. I can close my eyes and conjure up a beach on a hot day, imagine the warm sand under my feet, the sun on my face, the sound of waves; then, in a split second, I can change to a winter day on a mountain, with snow underfoot and on the branches of the trees, and a cold wind on my face . . . But Miller points out that the 'control panel' of such imaginings is the ego itself. *I* decide on the change of scene, and my imagination obliges.

What Miller is saying, in effect, is that the right brain is the orchestra and the left brain is the conductor. If, for example, I relax and read poetry, or listen to music, I can induce all kinds of moods, and eventually achieve a state in which I can change my mood instantly: I can turn, let us say, from Milton's *L'Allegro* to *Il Penseroso*, and conjure up with total realism a summer scene with merrymakers and then the 'dim religious light' of abbeys and churches and pinewoods. The right and left brains can eventually achieve the same relationship as a great conductor with his orchestra — the orchestra that has come to respond to his most delicate gesture. But such a state of harmony depends on the initial recognition that *I* am the conductor. *I* must take up my baton, tap the music stand, and say 'Gentlemen, today we do the Jupiter Symphony . . . ' The greatest danger of active imagination is that the subject should assume it means handing over his baton to the orchestra — which is obviously an absurdity. Active imagination is a state of cooperation in which the ego must remain the dominant partner.

Western man is in the position of a conductor who is unaware that he possesses an orchestra — or is only dimly and intermittently aware of it. Active imagination is a technique for becoming aware of the orchestra. This is 'individuation'. And it is clearly only a beginning. The next task is to develop a random collection of musicians into a great orchestra. *This* is the real task of the conductor. And this seems to be what Jung meant when he said, towards the end of his life: 'Consciousness is the supreme arbiter.'

Select Bibliography

Works by C.G. Jung

The Collected Works of C.G. Jung, 20 vols (Routledge and Kegan Paul)

Letters, selected and edited by Gerhard Adler, 2 vols (Routledge and Kegan Paul, 1976).

The Freud/Jung Letters, edited by William McGuire (Routledge and Kegan Paul, 1974).

Memories, Dreams, Reflections (Routledge and Kegan Paul, 1963).

Man and his Symbols with M-L von Franz, Joseph L. Henderson, Jolande Jacobi and Aniela Jaffé (Aldus, 1964).

Word and Image, edited by Aniela Jaffé, Bollingen Series (Princeton University Press, 1979).

C.G. Jung: Speaking, Interviews and Encounters, edited by William McGuire and R.F.C. Hull (Thames and Hudson, 1978).

Books on Jung

Bennet, E.A., *C.G. Jung* (Barrie and Rockcliffe, 1961).

Brome, Vincent, *Jung, Man and Myth* (Macmillan, 1978).

Franz, M-L von, *C.G. Jung, His Myth in Our Time* (Putnams, 1975).

Hannah, Barbara, *Encounters with the Soul: Active Imagination as developed by C.G. Jung* (Sigo Press, 1981).

Jaffé, Aniela, *From the Life and Work of C.G. Jung* (Hodder and Stoughton, 1972).

Post, Laurens van der, *Jung and the Story of Our Time* (The Hogarth Press, 1976).

Speigelman, J. Marvin, *The Knight* (Falcon Press, Phoenix, Arizona, 1982).

Index

Goethe, J.W. von, 14, 17, 21, 22, 24, 25, 30, 51, 65, 79, 95, 101, 120, 121, 123, 136
Golden Dawn, Hemetic Order of the, 10, 103, 106
Great Mother, 153
Greely, Horace, 136
Gurdjieff, G.I., 89, 131

Hall, Edward T., 90
Hannah, Barbara, 152-3
'Healing the Split', 122
Heart of Darkness, 99
Hegel, G.W.F., 124, 136
Herodotus, 57
Hippocrates, 115
Hölderlin, J.C.F., 65, 73, 76, 146
Hollandus, 102
homosexuality, 46, 90, 121
Hu Shih, 91
Hudson, Thomson Jay, 24-5, 31, 77-9, 81, 88, 131, 133, 139, 146
Human Comedy, 136
Hume, David, 142
Huxley, Aldous, 14
Huxley, T.H., 15, 65
Hyslop, J.H., 32

I Ching, 8-9, 15, 83, 88, 91, 95, 113, 114
Idiot, The, 141
Il Penseroso, 155
individuation, 87-9, 109, 137-40, 143, 147, 154-5
International Medical Society for Psychotherapy, 108
Interpretation of Dreams, 10, 42-3, 68
introvert type, 92-4

Jaffé, Aniéla, 104, 109, 112, 121
James, William, 32, 142
Janet, Pierre, 39-41, 43-4, 56, 62, 79, 110, 127-30, 133, 136
  and neurosis, 127-8, 133
Jaynes, Julian, 151
Jones, Ernest, 46, 57, 65
Jordan, Dr Furneaux, 92-4
Journal of Psychiatry, 35
Joyce, James, 109
Jung, Carl Gustav, 7-8, 15, 17-18, 25-6, 34-8, 41-2, 45-7, 51-2, 54, 57, 64, 66-70
  attack at school, 18
  and Christianity, 118-20
  death of, 123
  end of association with Freud, 66-70
  first meeting with Freud, 46-7
  and first signs of split personality, 22
  and Freud's sexual theory, 51-2, 58, 64, 76, 88
  and his father, 17
  and his mother, 17-18
  and his painting, 80-81, 85
  and hypnosis, 42
  and the *I Ching*, 91
  and interest in mythology, 58
  and interest in magic, 99
  and letter to Freud, 45
  and marriage, 41
  and near death experience, 7-8, 15
  and poltergeist in bookcase, 54
  and 'the round house', 96
  and word association tests, 36-7, 44, 57
  at Burghölzli Mental Hospital, 34-38, 57
  collected works of, 41, 135, 138, 145, 150
Jung, Emma, 46, 53-4, 58, 60, 71, 89, 96, 121
  correspondence with Freud, 60

Kali, 83

Kant, Immanuel, 22
Kardec, Allen, 28
Kepler, Johannes, 115
Kerner, Justinus, 30
Kierkegaard, Sören, 110
Knight, The, 153
Koestler, Arthur, 92
Krafft-Ebing, Baron Richard von, 11, 33, 51, 76

L'Allegro, 155
Lavoisier, Antoine-Laurent, 102
Law of Psychic Phenomena, The, 24, 31, 77
Lawrence, D.H., 97
Lawrence, T.E., 90
Leibniz, G.W. von, 115
L'Enfer, 146
Lindbergh, Charles, 117, 135
Long, Dr Constance, 93
Long, Max Freedom, 150
Luther, Martin, 95

Magnus, Albertus, 114
Man and his Symbols, 15
Man, Myth and Magic, 9
Mandala symbol, 31, 81, 83, 87-8, 100, 105, 117, 120
manic-depression, 36
Mann, Thomas, 135-6
Marjula, Anna, 152
Maslow, Abraham, 137, 141
Mayer, Robert, 96
Memories, Dreams, Reflections, 10, 25, 82, 121
Meredith, George, 71
Metamorphoses and Symbols of the Libido, 61
Miller, Howard, 154-5
Miller, Miss Frank, 61-3
Milton, John, 155
Mirandola, Pico della, 115
Mithras Liturgy, 58
Moltzer, Mary, 58
Mörike, Eduard, 65
Moser, Fanny, 13, 135
multiple personality, 38-9
Myers, Frederic, 28
mysterium coniunctions, 102
Mysterium Coniunctionis, 105, 107, 121

'Nature of the Psyche, The', 105
Newton, Sir Isaac, 83
Nietzsche, Friedrich Wilhelm, 25, 27, 41, 51, 65, 73, 76, 80, 83, 95, 101, 146
nominalism, 95
Norman, Sir Montagu, 36, 38, 131
Nostradamus, 9

Occult, The, 140
Oedipus complex, 49, 66-7, 71, 129
'On so-called Occult Phenomena', 38
On Synchronicity, 9, 113
Origen, 94, 118
Origin of Consciousness in the Breakdown of the Bicameral Mind, The, 151

Pappenheim, Bertha, 47, 50
Paracelsus, 106, 115, 134
Philalethes, 102
Philemon, 75, 77-81, 91, 111, 134, 153
Philosopher's Stone, The, 106
Philosophy of the Unconscious, The, 27
Philp, E.H., 137
Plato, 67
Poe, Edgar Allan, 146
Polynesian religion, 96
Prajapti, 81
Preiswerk, Emilie, 17-18